Jeremiah 29:12–14
**'You will seek me and find me when you
seek me with all your heart.'** (v13)

We begin a fresh journey today. It's one that will lead us to Christmas. It is a journey framed by the timeless Christmas message – journeying with others in search of God.

EDWJ is our daily point of departure on this journey. Our desire is that we learn to live in the footsteps of Jesus. Our struggle is always the relentless pressure to conform to the pattern of the world that surrounds us, a world that has abandoned God in so many ways (Rom. 12:2).

As we step out on this journey, from wherever our starting point may be, we can be reassured in the knowledge that God does not deliberately disguise Himself in an attempt to hide from us. In fact, it is we who most often discover we are attempting to hide from God because of our shame, pain and disappointment created by life choices (Gen. 3:9–10).

Jeremiah, who prophesied at the time of Judah's destruction by the Babylonians and their subsequent exile, tells us that God wants to be found. The obstacle is never the elusive nature of the Lord, but an issue with our own attitude.

So our journey will invite us to consider all the baggage we bring with us before offering us the opportunity to reflect on the degree to which our heart yearns for God, whilst identifying where obstacles remain that separate us from God's full embrace.

SCRIPTURE TO CONSIDER: Deut. 6:1–6; Prov. 8:17–21; Jer. 29:1–9; Acts 17:24–31.

AN ACTION TO TAKE: When planning any journey we recognise it will require persistence and we will discover many things. Are you willing to undertake this journey in search of God?

A PRAYER TO MAKE: 'Lord, I am grateful that You invite me to get to know You better each and every day. May my faith and friendship grow. Amen.'

Write to micha@edwj.org and I'll write back personally and in confidence as soon as I can.

Luggage

Luke 9:1–6
**'He told them: "Take nothing for the journey – no staff, no
bag, no bread, no money, no extra shirt."'** (v3)

We all prepare for a journey in different ways. On pilgrimage,
where we daily have to carry all our own luggage, it's best to
travel light. In some ways, what we insist on including in our
luggage will reveal a lot about where our security lies.

God invites us to place all our security, or trust, in Him (Prov. 3:5–6).
This is perhaps the steepest learning curve any one of us faces; moving
from self-reliance to God-dependence. Yet, that is truly the nature of
faith.

I recently had a fascinating conversation with the principal of
Liverpool College. In brief, he fears that education had been reduced
to little more than a mechanistic system to produce academic results.
His contention: educators needed to ask what their real desire and
purpose was, and what were they willing to settle for? A critical
question, as their answers lay the foundations for future society.**

Perhaps, as we seek to integrate our faith with our life, we'd do well
to consider who we are and what we really want from life? It may well
be something far more intangible than the material objectives we can
easily invest our time in chasing after.

This journey will necessarily invite us to ask questions of ourselves
as we determine the depth of friendship and the nature of the Christian
life our heart desires.

SCRIPTURE TO CONSIDER: Psa. 118:5–10; Prov. 19:20–23; John 6:25–40; Phil. 3:7–14.

AN ACTION TO TAKE: It might be helpful to consider a short course to stimulate
our thinking about what we want to do in life. Visit Waverley LEARN at edwj.
org/nd21-2nov to see online and face-to-face opportunities that might serve
your needs.

A PRAYER TO MAKE: 'Lord, help me to discover who I am and who I am to
become. Give me courage on this journey. Amen.'

**Hans van Mourik Broekman, *Full Life: Letters to My Students* ; *Confessions of a Headteacher:
Ruminations in Lockdown*

1 John 1:1–4

'We proclaim to you what we have seen and heard, so that you also may have fellowship with us. And our fellowship is with the Father and with his Son, Jesus Christ.' (v3)

Journeys introduce us to people we haven't met before. On pilgrimage, we encounter and engage with a group and experience things together. Travelling alone, we still interact with people along the way. All interaction offers both a learning and a sharing opportunity. Initially, this can be superficial as we seek to locate each other in a context we understand. Some enjoy the safety of familiarity and the reinforcement of shared values. Others are hungry for new insights, to explore perceptions drawn from different life experiences.

Fresh insights can challenge all we hold dear. Yet, on a journey, we cross borders and experience different cultures. We become acutely aware of contrasts with what we customarily love and embrace. In acknowledging differences, we're not denying our experience and understanding. Yet, in weighing what we hear and observe, that understanding can be enriched. Equally, others gain insights from journeying with us.

Personal testimony, our own story, grounds our beliefs in reality. It places them in a context that others can recognise, discovering how our faith works in everyday experience. It lays the foundation for community, which we are all invited to help shape and sustain. Differences need not divide us; they can deepen our appreciation and understanding of God, others and ourselves.

SCRIPTURE TO CONSIDER: Prov. 3:1–8; 16:1–9; Heb. 10:19–25; 12:1–2.

AN ACTION TO TAKE: It's very easy to get stuck talking with the same people. Why not invite someone you don't know that well at church to have coffee with you? Enter upon a fresh journey of discovery.

A PRAYER TO MAKE: 'Lord, help me to learn more about my faith in action as I listen to others share their experience of making sense of faith. Amen'

Luke 24:13–25
**'As they talked and discussed these things with each
other, Jesus himself came up and walked along with them;
but they were kept from recognising him.'** (vv15-16)

For most journeys we know our destination from the outset. We make many journeys daily. We visit a neighbour, drive to the shops or take the dog round the block. Most of the time, our mind is anywhere but present with us on our travels but captured by our next task or filled with unresolved issues we know we must settle.

Two disciples set out for Emmaus. Dismayed and confused by the events surrounding Jesus' death, they pay little attention to a stranger who joins them. They are amazed at the fact that He isn't preoccupied with recent events, assuming that what absorbed them absorbs everyone.

It's easy imagining that everyone is caught up with the same concerns as us. However, this is untrue and our concerns may not be of interest to those we pass unnoticed on our life journey. We are invited to pay closer attention to the strangers we encounter, for God is present everywhere, all the time. Heads down, caught up in the moment, we can miss Jesus in the routine busyness of life.

God continuously speaks to us, and is always actively involved in our lives. Yet, God's voice may not come from a familiar, or indeed obvious, place. It is our responsibility constantly to remind ourselves to look upward and outward, and away from the narrative that preoccupies our mind, demanding our full attention.

SCRIPTURE TO CONSIDER: Exod. 4:1–5; 1 Kings 17:7–16; Matt. 13:31–33; 1 Cor. 1:18–31.

AN ACTION TO TAKE: We instinctively get caught up in our own world. Yet, God has called us to serve His kingdom purpose. Let's remain vigilant as to what God is saying to us throughout our daily schedule.

A PRAYER TO MAKE: 'Lord, may I learn to keep one eye on You, whatever consumes my immediate attention in the daily routine of my life. Amen.'

Jeremiah 6:16–20

'Stand at the crossroads and look; ask for the ancient paths, ask where the good way is, and walk in it, and you will find rest for your souls. But you said, "We will not walk in it."' (v16)

For most of us, good intentions are less the problem than the distractions of life's realities that hijack the best of them! The wisdom of God's Word makes sense, yet is too often lost in the many demands of our day.

So, one response we can make is to declare our intention clearly at the start of each day as we embark on a journey we know in part, but which may well carry us into uncharted territory. I love this verse from Jeremiah and use the first part as the final prayer in my devotions. It's one I have committed to memory, and I return to it once I realise I'm distracted.

I never want to respond by refusing to walk in God's way, but there are times when I have to do battle to keep my heart pure. The flotsam and jetsam of my daily trek through life too often provoke reactions and thoughts that do not represent God's kingdom.

There is a challenge in practising the fruit of repentance and living the prayer of King David, 'Create in me a pure heart, O God, and renew a steadfast spirit within me' (Psa. 51:10). Yet, it offers a useful benchmark for our day. It's worth pausing and reflecting, and when necessary praying, both these words from Psalm 51, and repeating what I have taken as a prayer from Jeremiah.

Living every day with Jesus is no great mystery, but practical and achievable, and there are simple tools to help us achieve our ambition.

SCRIPTURE TO CONSIDER: Psa. 24; Matt: 5:1–12; James 3:13–18; 1 Pet. 1:17–25.

AN ACTION TO TAKE: Will you build a habit of starting each day's journey by saying this prayer from Psalm 51 humbly and sincerely? Benchmark your day and briefly consider the purity of your heart.

A PRAYER TO MAKE: 'Lord, help me to keep my heart pure wherever my day's journey leads me. Amen.'

Elevate your expectation and wonder

Advent at Waverley Abbey Trust

- Advent retreats for reflection and inspiration

- Devotional material, drawing you into deeper exploration of the season

- Advent themed evenings at Waverley Abbey House

- Books and online resources

To find out more visit
waverleyabbeyresources.org/advent

WAVERLEY ABBEY TRUST

Sunset

Isaiah 30:15–18

'This is what the Sovereign LORD, the Holy One of Israel, says: "In repentance and rest is your salvation, in quietness and trust is your strength, but you would have none of it."' (v15)

The close of our day is an excellent time to pause and reflect on where we've travelled in the past 24 hours. So much can happen in a day; so many encounters and experiences to review.

Just as at the start of the day we make our appeal to God before setting out, it is also useful to take a moment to place ourselves back into God's hands just before we lie down to sleep. I use the first part of Isaiah's words as a prayer to quieten my active mind and place God front and centre of my thoughts.

His prophecy comes at a troubling time as Israel face defeat and exile by the Assyrians. Yet, with all the turmoil, God invites them to wait, to be calm and to trust that all will be well.

Darkness can provoke much mental anguish, so it is good to pause and decide to entrust ourselves to God's care. We can actively declare that we choose quietly to leave everything in His hands and accept His assurance that we are safe, physically, emotionally and spiritually.

Establishing a regular approach to closing our day improves the quality of our sleep. Many wellbeing practitioners recommend a 30-minute wind-down process as a useful preparation for a good night's sleep. It prepares your body, mind and spirit for the night before you.* As you wind down, turn off all technology, reflect on the day gone by, read some devotional material,** and be silent for some moments.

SCRIPTURE TO CONSIDER: Exod. 33:12–23; Psa. 4:4–8; Eph. 2:1–18.

AN ACTION TO TAKE: What will it take to create a regular habit of winding down before going to bed? Will you establish this rhythm for your wellbeing?

A PRAYER TO MAKE: 'Lord, by waiting and by calm I shall be saved, in quiet and in trust my strength lies. Amen.' (Isa. 30:15, NABRE)

* edwj.org/nd21-6nov1

**I recommend *A Year with Selwyn Hughes*, available from edwj.org/nd21-56nov2

Amos 3:3–6
'Do two walk together unless they have agreed to do so?' (v3)

God can make me feel quite uncomfortable. I am very aware of the many fractures in my life. Scripture speaks of the power of the gospel to transform our lives (Rom. 12:2; 2 Cor. 5:17). Transformation means to change from one thing to something completely different, something better.

I find this challenging because I observe that much of my life appears to resist transformation. It looks a lot like it did twenty years ago with the same misgivings, doubts and obvious flaws in attitude and behaviour. Our growth in God can prove a source of discouragement as well as blessing.

However, like all good friendships, learning to 'walk together' is a challenge. There are difficult seasons, yet in persevering we demonstrate the value we place on this friendship. We may fall out, despair of the other person, even entertain unkind thoughts and speak disrespectfully of them to others, but the friendship proves more resilient because ultimately we prize it more highly than the difficulties it creates.

This is equally true of our friendship with God. This week we have compared our friendship with God to a journey. There will be periods of discomfort, disillusion and even despondency. But God knows how we are made (He made us, after all: Gen. 1:26-28) and never tires of us, tantrums and all.

The journey continues for as long as I agree to participate – blisters, sore feet and all!

SCRIPTURE TO CONSIDER: Psa. 51:10–17; 103:1–22; Rom. 7:14–25; Col. 3:1–3.

AN ACTION TO TAKE: We all face a variety of challenges in life. Many of these reach deep into our understanding of ourselves. Let's agree to walk in step with Jesus and deepen our friendship with God.

A PRAYER TO MAKE: 'Lord, You are my shepherd, You refresh and guide me on life's path. May I keep my eyes fixed on You. Amen.'

Jeremiah 29:4–14

'For I know the plans I have for you,' declares the LORD, 'plans to prosper you and not to harm you, plans to give you hope and a future.' (v11)

Words that sound so comforting were spoken at a time of Judah's greatest pain and confusion. Exiled to Babylon, defeated, humbled and apparently abandoned by God. Prosperity, hope and a future seemed far from assured. Yet, God promised this was simply a staging post on the essential course of their God experience.

On any journey, we require a compass to ensure we are headed in the right direction. When natural landmarks like the stars and planets are obscured, we need to place our confidence in a little magnetised needle, probably first invented by the Chinese.*

We too are in exile. We await the return of Jesus and the restoration of God's kingdom on earth. Our compass is the Holy Spirit, and He will always draw us back towards Jesus. For this to happen we need discernment, to pay attention to the Spirit's leading, to avoid the rocks that can shipwreck our lives. And if we feel we are already marooned on a desert isle, that same Holy Spirit will rescue those of us who call out for help and surrender to His leading.

This week, we shall look at the compass given by God to enable us to live every day with Jesus in confidence. It alone offers the framework that ensures our steps lead us ever closer towards God's heart. Such a compass is an essential part of any pilgrim's equipment if they intend safely to navigate their way along God's narrow path through life.

SCRIPTURE TO CONSIDER: Psa. 32:6–11; Isa. 11:1–5; John 5:31–44; 16:12–15.

AN ACTION TO TAKE: If we want to travel consistently in God's direction we must discern where the Holy Spirit is leading us. Are we ready to enter upon unfamiliar paths and place our confidence in God's leading?

A PRAYER TO MAKE: 'Lord, I want to walk on Your path for my life, guided by Your Holy Spirit. Help me to discern where Your Spirit leads me. Amen.'

* edwj.org/nd21-8nov

Psalm 62:5–8

'Yes, my soul, find rest in God; my hope comes from him.' (v5)

God's promise and purpose as we respond to His invitation is to meet us in our pursuit of inner peace; rest for our soul. The Centre for Mental Health, following a spending review, reported the cost of mental health difficulties at a record level of £119 billion in 2019–2020.* One reason Waverley Abbey, through its training programmes and products, seeks to support those struggling and those offering support to people wrestling with their mental health concerns.**

Every day, Jesus wants us to find peace – this lies at the very core of our personal friendship with God. This peace impacts four key aspects of our daily life experience: the Holy Spirit acts as our compass to enable us to make peace with God, ourselves, other people, and the circumstances we find ourselves in.

Life ebbs and flows. One moment God seems so distant and I feel alone and forlorn. Then a precious relationship has some problems: my partner, my children, my best friend. The path God invites us to walk along is to enable us to grow up into maturity in Christ, to become the very best expression of ourselves. Here we discover our rest is in God, who is always our rock, stable and secure (Psa. 62:7).

Over the rest of this week, we shall consider these four compass points and consider how we might both make our peace and learn to rest in the fullness of God, every day.

SCRIPTURE TO CONSIDER: Psa. 72:1–14; Dan. 10:7–19; Rom. 5:1–8; 14:12–19.

AN ACTION TO TAKE: Consider where you are in relation to God, yourself, others and your circumstances. Would you describe yourself as at peace?

A PRAYER TO MAKE: 'Lord, may I take time to learn to live by your compass, who is the Holy Spirit. Amen.'

* edwj.org/nd21-9nov1
** edwj.org/nd21-9nov2

Peace with God

Romans 8:5–11
'The mind governed by the flesh is death, but the mind governed by the Spirit is life and peace.' (v6)

Scripture is clear; we choose to live by the flesh or by the Spirit. The flesh, in essence, is to live from a worldly point of view. It excludes God, or at least reduces God to a pattern of belief to which we only pay lip service. Our mortal lives consist of an ongoing battle between flesh and the Spirit.

The Spirit of God invites us to become heavenly-minded (Col. 3:1–4). Here we grow in our consciousness of God's way, so very different to the ways of this world. God challenges our natural instincts, for His way is not born from the deployment of our constituent parts; our physical, emotional and rational, mortal makeup.

We become conscious that knowing God is not the process of a moment of enlightenment, but rather the consequence of a journey. In choosing Christ we self-enrol in 'a school of God's service'.*As such, we must do some work to bring our will into line with God's will. We do this using our will and voluntarily making choices. Here we learn how to manage our appetites, those natural desires promising to satisfy our felt needs.

By this means, we grow closer to God. We acknowledge that not all appetites are good for us, and any appetite that we indulge can itself displace God from the primary focus of our life. The Holy Spirit always seeks to lead us into the very presence of God and to live out of the deposit of faith within us (1 Tim. 6:20).

SCRIPTURE TO CONSIDER: Psa. 119:1–16; Deut. 30:11–20; Rom. 8:9–17; 1 Cor. 2:9–16.

AN ACTION TO TAKE: The Bible is clear that following Jesus engages us in a battle of wills; my will or God's will. These battles occur daily, in our experience. Am I ready to fight to find God's will for my life?

A PRAYER TO MAKE: 'Lord, You invite me to choose between Your will or my will. I desire to follow You, but I face many battles. Lord, come to my aid in the thick of each battle. Amen.'

*The Rule of Saint Benedict, (London: SPCK, 1931), Prologue v45 edwj.org/nd21-10nov

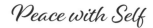

Ephesians 2:11–18

'For he himself is our peace, who has made the two groups one and has destroyed the barrier, the dividing wall of hostility.' (v14)

Finding 'inner peace' is the express longing of many people. Life not only makes physical demands, but also emotional and psychological. Whilst we turn to sleep to recharge our tired body, we may lie awake for hours unable to wind down within. Peace with God is closely related to peace with self. There are positive steps we can adopt. We can acknowledge both our inner turmoil and, when known, its cause. Then, choose to turn to God, the source of peace and acceptance. This may require work as we are consistently hijacked by our anxieties. Finally, we can talk with family and friends, those who know and love us and whom we trust. Sometimes they may guide us towards some appropriate, professional help.*

As disciples, God has granted us access to the One who knows us inside out, for He created us. Only as we find inner peace can we fully embrace life. We discover our security in God and accept who we are; the good, the bad and the indifferent. We are not perfect, but by God's grace we are invited to grow towards perfection (Matt. 5:48).

In a world in which every aspect of our outer and inner persona is scrutinised, how wonderful that we are accepted by God for who we are, not for who we might like to be. So we can be comfortable with who we are and then learn to grow in personal confidence and find all that's needed for a fulfilling life.

SCRIPTURE TO CONSIDER: Isa. 41:8–20; Psa. 119:161–168; Rom. 8:18–39; Luke 12:1–7.

AN ACTION TO TAKE: Learning to accept ourselves with the openness and generosity with which God welcomes us is often complex. Do we have the courage to learn to love ourselves, warts and all?

A PRAYER TO MAKE: 'Lord, thank You for loving me unconditionally. May I learn to see myself through Your accepting eyes of love. Amen.'

*Consider contacting the Association of Christian Counsellors (acc-uk.org/), or phone Premier's Lifeline (+44 (0)300 1110101) to speak to someone

Mark 12:28–31

'Love the Lord your God with all your heart and with all your soul and with all your mind and with all your strength. The second is this: "Love your neighbour as yourself." There is no commandment greater than these.' (vv 30–31)

Yesterday was Remembrance Day in the UK. My only childhood experience of church was attending Remembrance Sunday with my dad as he recalled fallen comrades Jesus is clear; failure to love neighbours is to fail to love God. We can present a host of reasons why this is impossible, but Jesus tells us we must love even our enemies (Matt. 5:44).

Whilst we might avoid and speak ill of others, we know people get under our skin. Our wellbeing is best served in preventing thoughts stirred by our disappointment in others from determining our attitude, and subsequently our view of life, and our place in it. We live in an age wracked with insecurity. We crowd together around certain 'norms' that society advances as evidence of 'the good life'. However, returning to the pages of Scripture we observe how the disciples lived. Jesus was always precise in His teaching (Matt. 18:1–10). We are to ask ourselves why we are reacting, rather than level blame at others. We cannot determine how others live their life, yet we exercise complete control, by God's grace, over how we order our own. My father opened my eyes to the value of treating others well.

SCRIPTURE TO CONSIDER: Lev. 19:11–19; Deut. 10:17–22; Matt. 7:7–14; 1 John 4:16–21.

AN ACTION TO TAKE: Loving others is a significant challenge. Love is neither avoidance nor rejection. Love is always a sober assessment of my own reactions and subsequent actions. Can I learn neighbour-love by God's grace?

A PRAYER TO MAKE: 'Lord, love never fails. Help me to build a love that is robust and resilient, a love that reflects the love You have for me. Amen.' (see 1 Cor. 13:4–13)

John 16:31–33
'I have told you these things, so that in me you may have peace. In this world you will have trouble. But take heart! I have overcome the world.' (v33)

Everyone experiences both triumph and tragedy in their life. Circumstances invade uninvited, and often unwelcome. At Waverley Abbey we are contacted by many people looking for encouragement through difficult experiences that test faith. They can fuel spiritual growth; they also provide the rocks on which our faith may become shipwrecked for a season.

Whilst we may read testimonies of those who have charted courses through troubling times, they cannot *practically* assist us in our times of trouble. We may draw encouragement, unearth a faith principle to apply, but we are on our own unique journey.

The good news is that the Holy Spirit is always with us (Rom. 8:26–27). God doesn't abandon us. We find it difficult to discern God in our circumstances (John 6:16–20), but as we persevere we find Jesus. He had always been with us; we just couldn't see Him through the challenges, external and internal, that we faced.

Learning to live at rest even as life appears to fall apart is indeed an act of faith. Yet, it is also a witness to a watching world, for we flesh out through experience what we confidently affirm when describing Jesus as Saviour and Lord (2 Tim. 1:12).

As Selwyn Hughes was fond of saying, 'Those who doubt most, and yet strive to overcome their doubts, turn out to be some of Christ's strongest disciples'.*

SCRIPTURE TO CONSIDER: Psa. 27; Isa. 41:17–20; Dan. 10:1–21; 1 Pet. 5:6–10.

AN ACTION TO TAKE: How might you practise keeping your gaze fixed on Jesus rather than on the changing circumstances of your daily life?

A PRAYER TO MAKE: 'Lord, I recognise that it is through the fires of life's many troubles that I can choose to grow my understanding of the life of faith to which I'm called. Amen.'

*Selwyn Hughes, *A Year with Selwyn Hughes* (Farnham: CWR, 2011) edwj.org/nd21-13nov

Ephesians 5:6–20

'Be very careful, then, how you live – not as unwise but as wise, making the most of every opportunity, because the days are evil. Therefore do not be foolish, but understand what the Lord's will is.'

(vv15–17)

As we learn to walk God's way, the Holy Spirit acts as our compass to ensure we learn to live our mortal life well. Christianity is both belief and behaviour. We discover that God empowers us to manage our daily life experience. This involves our inner world influenced by perception and emotion, as well as the way we interact through participation in the physicality of life.

Such management hinges upon our decision-taking. God recognises we are subject to the impact others have on our life, which can prove devastating. Yet, God also awakens us to the truth that we can make decisions for our own life. Those decisions will be influenced by the impact life has on us – informing our mind, our feelings and our attitudes. But, with God we are invited to listen to the Spirit's voice and take the brave decision to explore what it means to live under God's governance.

It takes courage to live for God, obeying His Spirit, as Scripture reveals. Abraham set out on a journey, destination unknown, in his retirement years, whilst Jeremiah gave up his independence. Both said yes to God. In a world in which 'self-actualisation' is strongly advocated, God asks us to humble ourselves, to surrender our independence and choose to serve God's purpose first and foremost, even when we cannot see its purpose or benefits. This faith is reflected in our decisions and the fruit of our lives.

SCRIPTURE TO CONSIDER: Deut. 26:16–27:9; Jer. 7:20–29; Acts 5:25–42; 1 John 2:3–6.

AN ACTION TO TAKE: It is a challenge we face every day: will we take decisions that reflect God's will or our own preferences? This will depend on the confidence we have in God's compass for life.

A PRAYER TO MAKE: 'Lord, strengthen my resolve to make decisions that reflect Your purpose so that my life may produce kingdom fruit. Amen.'

3 John 2–4

'Dear friend, I pray that you may enjoy good health and that all may go well with you, just as you are progressing spiritually.' (v2)

We seek to live lives of generosity. All too often, our best of intentions is hijacked by a distant, painful memory, or an unfair, instant judgment. I am bemused with both the enthusiasm I have for God's way, and my often complete ignorance in walking in Jesus' footsteps.

It is encouraging to discover how God equips us with a compass, a metaphorical aid to navigating the Christian life. We are encouraged to use this compass for two essential purposes.

First, there is a balance between its four points. If I engage too much with God, I instinctively distance myself from the other points: self, neighbours and circumstances. There's a chance I become too heavenly-minded, and fail to live the God-life in practice. The same can be said whenever we focus too intently on any one of the points; we become self-absorbed, implicated too closely in the lives of others or consumed with the reality of our circumstances.

It's best to take a balanced and measured view, and live equidistant from each of the points. When here, and it is a difficult space to occupy continuously, I have perspective on the critical areas of my daily life.

Second, I use it as a template for reviewing and praying into my day. Here it offers us the opportunity to consider how we are dealing with our walk of faith. The fruit of our reflection will then feed and focus us on the journey for the next day of challenge.

SCRIPTURE TO CONSIDER: Isa. 30:20–26; Micah 4:1–5; Luke 10:38–42; 2 Cor. 5:1–10.

AN ACTION TO TAKE: If useful to you, consider using this compass to help you walk in God's ways. Audit your life in the light of God's Word as revealed through Scripture.

A PRAYER TO MAKE: 'Lord, I want to establish a balanced approach to living the Christian life. Please help me. Amen.'

Let's Reason Together

Isaiah 1:16–20

"'Come now, let us settle the matter," says the LORD. "Though your sins are like scarlet, they shall be as white as snow; though they are red as crimson, they shall be like wool."' (v18)

God can seem like a great idea, but an unrealisable aspiration. A sense that we are loved by the creator of our world touches our emotions, yet our minds tell us this is only an idle dream.

The Bible is full of God's invitations to fractured humanity to step into His loving embrace. In the various pandemic lockdowns, many wrote of their sense of forlorn isolation. Some were driven to suicide, overwhelmed by a collapse in both confidence and any sense of belonging. Life isn't easy. It confronts us with apparently insurmountable challenges; seasons when we wrestle with past ghosts, or gaze at ourselves only to see our ragged edges.

God recognises that we can't do anything for ourselves (John 15:5). But He has created a home of hospitality for all those at their wits end and desperately seeking fresh hope (Isa. 55:1). Whilst such things might appear to defy reason, what if there was a God who was accessible and who wanted to support us in making our lives work? 'Come let us reason together', is God's invitation to each one of us. It's a simple conversation starter, and who hasn't experienced a simple conversation leading to something we could never have imagined or anticipated?

The only reason we find ourselves on the Christian journey is because we responded to such an invitation. Yet, we are not part of an exclusive club. God is accessible to all. The point of departure is the moment we agree, often with many reservations, to take God at His word and start that conversation.

SCRIPTURE TO CONSIDER: Job 22:21–30; Isa. 55:6–13; John 3:16–21; Col. 1:15–23.

AN ACTION TO TAKE: The question we all face is, what's to be gained by seeking God's friendship? The better question is, what do we have to lose? Respond to God's invitation to talk things through.

A PRAYER TO MAKE: 'Lord, please hear my voice and cleanse me from my sin. Amen.'

Hosea 6:1–6

'Come, let us return to the LORD. He has torn us to pieces but he will heal us; he has injured us but he will bind up our wounds.' (v1)

J esus' earthly life reveals that no one can avoid pain. As we age we observe, and draw encouragement from the fact that many build their testimony to God's presence in life's storms. When trauma strikes, we seek to defend ourselves as best we can. Most often, those closest to us bear the burden of our reaction, a product of pain and shame. Maybe we're safest with those we bleed all over; or that they choose and refuse to distance themselves when confronted with the brutality of our lostness and grief.

Trials are no guarantee of maturing faith, but are guaranteed to shake us to the core. We feel all we've entrusted to God, our faith and service, counts for nothing. We're then tempted to blame God. Good news, God can absorb our worst reactions; I say that as one who collapsed beneath the weight of my greatest trial.

My shame dissipated as I accepted I was simply unravelling and I gasped in wonder at discovering how God loves me at my absolute worst. When I felt most alone – abandoned by those I needed, yet whom I most likely had driven from my side through my despicable behaviour – God was there. Very slowly, with reluctance and uncertainty, I chose to 'return to the Lord'. I was gently healed and, whilst I still carry the scars and walk with a limp, I love God in a way I had never previously known. Each of us can find this road of return to God's never-ending love, although we may find it hard to recognise the person God moulds from the tears and ashes of our bitter experiences.

SCRIPTURE TO CONSIDER: Psa. 34:4–18; 147:1–11; 2 Cor. 1:3–11; 1 Pet. 4:12–19.

AN ACTION TO TAKE: Can you accept that, at your very worst, God still loves you? We are not defined by our mistakes, but by God's confidence in us and the faith we choose to place in God.

A PRAYER TO MAKE: 'Lord, thank You that You bind up my wounds and heal my deepest pain. Amen.'

Matthew 11:25–30

'Come to me, all you who are weary and burdened, and I will give you rest. Take my yoke upon you and learn from me, for I am gentle and humble in heart, and you will find rest for your souls.' (vv28–29)

At times, we feel the weight of life heavy upon our shoulders. It takes the edge off everything. There are remedies, many quite debilitating. Those in management roles tell me they get home and reach for a glass of wine to relax them. I'm not critical, I've had my flirtations with alcohol dependence, both the buzz and to quieten my anxiety.

Burden is an idea that originates from the drone we associate with bees. What starts as a background sound we can easily ignore, eventually dominates and becomes all we can hear, interrupting our peace of mind and the focus of every waking moment.

Any of us can be subject to a dominant theme that grows into an intolerable burden to wear us down. Many marriages lose their way, distance grows between child and parent, work pressures no longer lift on our commute home.

Again God invites us to respond to His invitation to lay our burdens on Him. In exchange, we yoke ourselves to God so that now we work in concert in managing them better. Whilst solutions aren't immediately apparent, we can find confidence, despite our worst fears, and experience inner peace.

This is a process we improve as we move through life. We can learn to exchange fear and anxiety for the presence of God as we are joined in heart with our loving Father.

SCRIPTURE TO CONSIDER: Psa. 55:1–8,16–22; 145:14–21; Phil. 4:6–9; 1 Pet. 5:5–10.

AN ACTION TO TAKE: Are the ways you process life's stress points healthy? Do you find Jesus a source of help in alleviating such stress? Consider a day course with Waverley Abbey. edwj.org/nd21-18nov

A PRAYER TO MAKE: 'Lord, teach me to bring my burdens to You daily, and find my promised rest. Amen.'

Beyond Death

Acts 4:8–14

'Salvation is found in no one else, for there is no other name under heaven given to mankind by which we must be saved.' (v12)

Salvation means to be rescued from danger, loss and harm. Mum always advised me to keep out of harm's way, words I frequently failed to heed. We're wired to seek safety ahead of danger; an instinct that grows stronger as we age. Today I'm more risk averse and aware of potential dangers than ever.

One unanswerable question is, what lies beyond death? Society treats death as our Victorian forbears dealt with sex – best not discussed. Today we have sexualised every aspect of our world, yet there is an awkwardness in talking about our inevitable end of life. We have attempted to medicate it, and hope that some professional will deal with the process that sees us depart this world.

Advances in medicine are all weighted to offer promises of interventions to extend mortal existence. Yet, Scripture declares that death is never the problem, it's what happens next (Rom. 14:7–9)? Once we accept God's invitation in Christ and take hold of salvation, we discover death itself is subject to God's authority; it is merely the vehicle to carry us into God's presence, our eternal rest.

But if we have doubts about the validity of God's invitation, or His ability to make good on His promise, death will prove daunting. As with every invitation, it's only through acceptance and participation that we can experience the reality of all that invitation promises.

SCRIPTURE TO CONSIDER: Eccl. 12:1–7; Isa. 25:6–9; John 5:19–30; Phil. 1:15–26.

AN ACTION TO TAKE: Is the thought of death something you avoid because it discomforts you? Reflect on God's promise to accompany you through your mortal life and lead you into the presence of God.

A PRAYER TO MAKE: 'Lord, thank You that as I accept your invitation to love and serve you my life is safe in Your hands, both now and into my future. Amen.'

Psalm 34:1–3
'Glorify the LORD with me: let us exalt his name together.' (v3)

God's infinitude is mirrored in the countless ways we can choose to meet Him. It's easy to fall into a habitual style in our approach to God. However, we know that relationships can waste away when treated as a duty, for familiarity breeds contempt. Both individually, and as congregations, we are invited to 'grasp how wide and long and high and deep is the love of Christ, and to know this love that surpasses knowledge' (Eph. 3:18–19a). As we explore our relationship with God we discover more of that 'measure of all the fullness of God' (Eph. 3:19b).

Time can be our greatest enemy in this regard. With so much to do every day, how are we to make the time to encounter God? We are all constructed differently and will therefore develop different paths along which to travel to meet with God.

Whilst privileged with so many resources (increasingly available online) to encourage our friendship with the Lord, God still invites us to build a pattern, a lifestyle, within which this rich relationship might grow. God's objective is that everything else falls into shadow in the light of His acceptance and love (Heb. 1:3).

In a similar way to how we focus on building our career, our material security and our family life, God asks us to establish deeper friendship with Himself; one that grows every day, and deepens our faith.

SCRIPTURE TO CONSIDER: Gen. 4:1–7; Psa. 34:4–22; Rom. 8:31–39; Eph. 1:3–14.

AN ACTION TO TAKE: When you consider life, whilst there are sources of anxiety, remember to give thanks to God for who He is, not just for what He does.

A PRAYER TO MAKE: 'Lord, I lift up my voice and give You praise and thanks for Your boundless love for me. Amen.'

Revelation 3:19–22
'Here I am! I stand at the door and knock. If anyone hears my voice and opens the door, I will come in and eat with that person, and they with me.' (v20)

This past week we have identified some of the overtures God makes in inviting us to follow Him, whatever our circumstances or presence of mind. Yet, even if we turn a blind eye and reject them, God will never give up on us. His whole purpose is to seek and find us and bring us back into friendship through the Spirit (Luke 15:3–7).

In our darkest moments God is always standing at the threshold of our heart, but we alone have the authority to invite someone across the doorstep. Indeed, it's said that an Englishman's home is his castle, and may explain the English reserve so often related by visitors to the country. However, if we simply open the door, God will step in and talk with us.

Throughout the Gospel accounts, knowledge of Jesus began at the meal table (for instance, Mark 2:15–17). God's first commitment is to welcome and converse with us. All decisions about the truth of Jesus' gospel message lie within our gift. We either choose to respond, and take God's revelation for a road test, or reject God's invitation altogether. There's no neutral territory. Jesus has the capability to divide people. I have made my choice and choose to follow Jesus, despite my doubts and fears. How about you? Don't sit on the fence. Make the choice to invite Jesus in, begin a conversation and go for a test drive.

SCRIPTURE TO CONSIDER: Isa. 62:11–12; Ezek. 34:7–16; Luke 19:1–10; John 14:15–21.

AN ACTION TO TAKE: Recall those moments when you have sensed God knocking at the threshold of your life. Will you turn and welcome Him in?

A PRAYER TO MAKE: 'Lord, thank You that You never stop seeking to find and establish a relationship with us. Amen.'

Write to micha@edwj.org and I'll write back personally and in confidence as soon as I can.

Matthew 4:18–22

'"Come, follow me," Jesus said, "and I will send you out to fish for people." At once they left their nets and followed him.' (vv19–20)

ow many of us know we have received this direct invitation from Jesus: 'follow me'? These two simple words are found 13 times in the Gospels. In response, the first disciples left what they were doing and chose Jesus.

Choosing Jesus is one thing, yet that very decision carries with it a commitment to continue wherever Jesus leads. Clearly we surrender our will and choose actively to obey God rather than any other authority. For those first disciples it had implications for families, businesses and how they were perceived within their community. There were moments of choice, such as when they abandoned Jesus ahead of His crucifixion (Mark 14:50). This a stark reminder that following Jesus is organic, always subject to change and development.

This remains every disciple's challenge, consistently responding to Jesus' invitation to follow. There is obviously a starting point, but Christianity is an immersive process; we journey ever deeper into our understanding, appreciation and service of God (Matt. 16:24–25). We need to be 'all in' and it's a challenge. I've stagnated at times in my Christian journey, only to discover God is as patient as He is insistent. Every point of pause offers a fresh opportunity where we're invited to say yes or no to God. Each pause presents a fresh occasion to renew and grow our faith muscle.

SCRIPTURE TO CONSIDER: Isa. 48:16–19; Num. 14:17–25; Luke 9:18–27; John 14:15–21.

AN ACTION TO TAKE: How difficult do you find walking in Jesus' footsteps every day? You have the power to press pause or play – which will it be?

A PRAYER TO MAKE: 'Lord, thank You for your patience. I want to rise up and follow You every moment of every day. Help me to exercise my faith muscle. Amen.'

Amos 5:4–5

'Seek me and live; do not seek Bethel, do not go to Gilgal, do not journey to Beersheba. For Gilgal will surely go into exile, and Bethel will be reduced to nothing.' (vv4–5)

What makes for the good life? There are many recipes on offer. Background, peer pressure and, increasingly, media play a significant part in shaping our opinion. It takes a self-assured individual to stand their ground on things they believe to be best for their life in the face of noisy opposition.

I best demonstrate what's good for me through the choices I take in practising that good. It takes courage and confidence to face criticism and perhaps be in the minority. Jesus demonstrates the way we can do this with His life of grace and kindness.

God's promise is that in seeking Him we shall find life (Prov. 8:17). Israel's Old Testament history reveals a people who were invited frequently to seek and serve God. Yet, even those places where God was manifest were emptied of God's glory through disobedience and neglect. Whilst the people followed their religious observances much as their ancestors had, all they held onto were rules of ritual devoid of God's presence.

It's so easy to lose hold of God in life, or to lose confidence in God's love and commitment to us. Each new day demands that we seek God afresh. It is only by seeking God that we can find Him. God invites us to search for Him, whilst promising He can always be found. There's a danger that we assume we have all the time in the world; but will we use that time well or simply fritter it away? Let's not get distracted, but positively seek God every day.

SCRIPTURE TO CONSIDER: Deut. 4:15–31; 1 Chron. 16:7–14; Matt. 6:19–24; Luke 11:5–13.

AN ACTION TO TAKE: Opening Scripture and praying offers us a reminder that our life is directed towards seeking God. Start each day with a prayer renewing your commitment to seek God.

A PRAYER TO MAKE: 'Lord, thank You that each day presents a fresh opportunity to go in search of You. I choose to seize that opportunity today. Amen.'

Fully Committed

2 Chronicles 16:7–9

'For the eyes of the LORD range throughout the earth to strengthen those whose hearts are fully committed to him. You have done a foolish thing, and from now on you will be at war.' (v9)

It might seem a considerable demand to request a heart fully committed to God. In the past, I've assumed it's what I *do* for God that somehow establishes my Christian credentials. Yet, in a season when I was brought very low, I found God present regardless of my inability to do anything. I was 27 and collapsed with physical exhaustion. Full commitment is made up of surrender, seeking, sitting and serving.

Surrender is a recognition that we are completely at another's mercy. It's all too easy to surrender parts, but not all of our life. Or to negotiate terms for our surrender. There are no terms but complete capitulation to God.

From a place of submission, in which we voluntarily choose to hold nothing back from God, we go in search of what's available in this place of surrender. How are we to live, since all we've known we have surrendered? Seeking God is the fundamental activity of a committed disciple learning to live under God's instruction.

Then we sit, realising that in fact God invites us to wait on Him. We do this in prayer, for prayer accompanies us throughout our day (1 Thess. 5:17). We discover how to sit with God, whether active or resting. Developing this sense of God's continuous presence deepens our hunger to search for more of God.

Finally, we serve, for we see clearly who we are in God and how God has formed us to represent His purposes on earth in the best way we can.

SCRIPTURE TO CONSIDER: Psa. 32; 27; Matt. 6: 25–34; Luke 10:38–42.

AN ACTION TO TAKE: Explore when and how you can build your daily life and time style around surrender, seeking, sitting and serving.

A PRAYER TO MAKE: 'Lord, help me to live my life fully committed to You. Amen.'

God is Great

Psalm 40:16–17

'But may all who seek you rejoice and be glad in you; may those who long for your saving help always say, "The LORD is great!"' (v16)

Augustine of Hippo writes, 'there will come days of tribulations, and greater tribulations...Let no-one promise himself what the gospel does not promise'.* We do not give thanks for an avoidance of trouble; we give thanks to God for provision through the trouble itself. It's what Walter Brueggemann helpfully describes as, 'the move from disorientation to new orientation'.**

It's common to think of human life as a straight line from emergence to departure. Yet, our path meanders in many different and distinct directions as life unfolds. Expectation first fragments, and then perishes on the rocks of our fears; we must carefully explore if we are to discover the pearl buried deep in the dirt (Matt. 13:45–46).

It is a challenge to keep going. Putting on a brave face can only briefly help. We must rather put on brave hearts, and these can only be crafted by the work of the Spirit within (Deut. 31:6). As with all enduring works, this is not the product of a momentary encounter with God, but the fruit of a well developed friendship.

We are privileged to know the end of God's redemptive and recovery narrative. Learning to live with the end in view may prove costly, but being dedicated to God's deliverance implies entrusting ourselves to our dependable Lord. This can inspire a song in our heart and a spring in our step.

SCRIPTURE TO CONSIDER: Deut. 7:17–26; Jer. 12:1–4; Mark 4:1–20; 1 Pet. 5:6–11.

AN ACTION TO TAKE: The word *courage* means heart, the core of our being.*** Can you find the courage to see you through and develop a state of mind rooted in God and God's Word?

A PRAYER TO MAKE: 'Lord, give me the courage to dig in the dirt to unearth the pearls of Your grace. Amen.'

*Augustine of Hippo, 'Expositions on the Book of Psalms'. **Walter Brueggemann, *The Message of the Psalms* (Minneapolis, MN: Augsberg, 1984) p131

Commend God Together

Psalm 145:3–7

'One generation commends your works to another; they tell of your mighty acts. They speak of the glorious splendour of your majesty – and I will meditate on your wonderful works. They tell of the power of your awesome works – and I will proclaim your great deeds.' (vv4–6)

Lockdown reintroduced us to isolation. Normal social life was overnight replaced with living under our own roof, with workplace, shops and cafés no longer available. Many found they struggled with their health and wellbeing.

Community is born in God. As Trinity – Father, Son and Holy Spirit – there is a togetherness at the heart of God. The Church reflects this communal life. Society, however, tends to celebrate self-realisation, emphasising the essential nature of the individual within society.

There is always a fundamental question about the individual's ability to care for themself or to need others' help. What is the role and responsibility of government, welfare and other mediating structures in crafting a healthy society? The debate rolls on, but not here!

When isolated, we can recall that we are just the latest generation to go in search of God. We have ample testimony from previous generations of His faithfulness. One thing no one else can do for us is to contemplate what such testimony means for today. Have we outgrown a need for a god?

Clearly not, given the fragile state of many individuals challenged through long periods of lockdown. This, in part, can be addressed through specialist services, themselves sadly in short supply. Also, by creating hospitable spaces through existing church communities. Something God invites us to do together.

SCRIPTURE TO CONSIDER: Psa. 133; 145:8–21; Acts 2:40–47; Rom. 12:3–21.

AN ACTION TO TAKE: Drawing inspiration from God's works throughout history, can your church community offer hope in your locality? Take a look at *God's Plan for Your Wellbeing*, to draw people together locally: edwj.org/nd21-26nov

A PRAYER TO MAKE: 'Lord, thank You for the stories of Your faithfulness that build my faith, and may I share them with my community. Amen.'

Understanding

Proverbs 2:1–8

'Indeed, if you call out for insight and cry aloud for understanding, and if you look for it as for silver and search for it as for hidden treasure, then you will understand the fear of the LORD and find the knowledge of God.' (vv3–5)

U nderstanding comes from God, and we are invited to go in search of it. Once we understand something we are able to make sense of it, both for ourselves and others. Peter declares, 'But in your hearts revere Christ as Lord. Always be prepared to give an answer to everyone who asks you to give the reason for the hope that you have. But do this with gentleness and respect' (1 Pet. 3:15).

To do this we must take time to understand our faith. This is why reading Scripture daily is essential, for within its pages we have God revealing the truth about Himself and His kingdom. We may struggle at points, but there are materials to help us.* These enable us to get a clearer and deeper understanding of our faith.

This is important for two reasons. First, it ensures that we develop our personal understanding of who God is and how we might live every day with Jesus practically and effectively. Second, we are able to share our faith with others and answer their questions intelligently and helpfully.

Building our understanding does take work, for it is a 'hidden treasure' only discovered by those with a hunger for God. Faith is indeed nurturing this hunger so that we might continuously be in search of a greater understanding of God in our life, and then how we might serve God effectively. We seek God to grow in our understanding and strengthen our faith for all that life throws at us.

SCRIPTURE TO CONSIDER: Psa. 119:9–20; Neh. 8:1–8; Luke 24:36–49; Rom. 10:14–21.

AN ACTION TO TAKE: Find a suitable resource to help you understand God's Word. How confident are you in explaining your faith?

A PRAYER TO MAKE: 'Lord, please open my eyes when reading Your Word so that I will grow in understanding. Amen.'

*See our range of reasonably priced *Cover to Cover* Bible guides: edwj.org/nd21-27nov

1 Thessalonians 5:16–24
'May God himself, the God of peace, sanctify you through and through. May your whole spirit, soul and body be kept blameless at the coming of our Lord Jesus Christ.' (v23)

Today is the first day of Advent. It introduces our seasonal Christmas preparation. Known as the lesser fast, it offers disciples an opportunity to prepare their hearts for Jesus; not simply focusing upon remembering the incarnation, but more looking towards Christ's return (Mark 13:26).

The subject of Christ's return is not much talked about today, yet offers a significant reason for obeying Jesus. In our busyness, it's easy to get caught up in the moment. Christmas increases the intensity as we seek to organise for what's a long public holiday. It's a season when we can quickly forget God in the rush.

Focusing on Christ's inevitable return, we get a better perspective on life, reminded that our life is lived in celebration of the promises realised through the incarnation, and fulfilled at Christ's second coming.

So these days of Advent offer us an opportunity to invest some time and energy to consider how our lives reflect the character and promise of God on earth. It's a tremendous time for witness as almost everyone still retains some idea of the biblical story of Christmas.

Visit edwj.org/nd21-28nov, and discover resources to support you in your journey to Christmas. If Waverley Abbey is near your home, invite your neighbours and friends to our carols and mince pie event in the House.

SCRIPTURE TO CONSIDER: Luke 21:5–36; Acts 1:6–11; 2 Pet. 3:1–18; Rev. 21:1–8.

AN ACTION TO TAKE: Take this season of Advent and make it an opportunity to reflect on the source of our salvation, born in Bethlehem; begin to look forward to Christ's return and live with that in view.

A PRAYER TO MAKE: 'Lord, come and renew my hope and vision of Your saving grace. Amen.'

Mark 13:32–37

'Be on guard! Be alert! You do not know when that time will come. It's like a man going away: he leaves his house and puts his servants in charge, each with their assigned task, and tells the one at the door to keep watch.' (vv33–34)

The incarnation, the event that we celebrate each Christmas, was a surprise to all but God. Mary was invited by an angel to give herself to God in the divine conception of Jesus. She had no foreknowledge, and enjoyed little time to decide if to agree or not.

With God, history can radically change direction in a moment. Our human instinct is to procrastinate, to sit on the fence, and weigh up pros and cons ahead of any decision. God seeks to move a little faster than that. Did God know Mary would say yes? In one way He did, because God is omniscient. Yet, equally, each of us is given free will to decide for ourselves the degree to which we pursue God (Gen. 2:15-17).

The danger is that we are lulled into a false security that one day will follow the next as surely as the sun rises each morning. However, God is Lord of all and has the authority to order things to direct humanity's attention to His purpose in history. The Old Testament provides a record that God's patience eventually reaches an end, when His chosen refuse to follow His directions and realise 'the goodness of the LORD in the land of the living' (Psa. 27:13–14).

We are pilgrims here on earth (Heb. 11:13), and must be alert for we are in a foreign country, conscious that we are here to represent God and not live for personal achievements.

SCRIPTURE TO CONSIDER: Psa. 39:7–13; Jer. 50:4–7; Phil. 3:7–21; Heb. 11:8–19.

AN ACTION TO TAKE: In the routine of life, are you aware of times when you felt God asked something of you but you chose to dismiss it? Revisit such moments and ask God to speak as the angel spoke to Mary.

A PRAYER TO MAKE: 'Lord, may I live a life worthy of You and please You in every way: bearing fruit in every good work whilst growing in the knowledge of God. Amen.' (from Col. 1:10)

1 Corinthians 3:1–9

'What, after all, is Apollos? And what is Paul? Only servants, through whom you came to believe – as the Lord has assigned to each his task. I planted the seed, Apollos watered it, but God has been making it grow.' (vv5–6)

The word Advent is from the Latin, one meaning is 'glorious arrival', speaking of the incarnation, and Christ's future return. For each of us there is some arrival point where we encounter Christ; the time at which we choose to follow God's way in how we live our life.

Paul points out that it is not the context within which we encounter Christ, nor the process we follow to enter into fellowship with God's people, but rather the degree to which the seed of Christian discipleship is enabled to grow that is important. It's all too easy to become sidetracked with Christian personalities or style. This is only for the fashion conscious, for we are summoned to a far greater opportunity to know and serve God every day.

Remarkably, we are each invited to make our own journey to Jesus' crib each Christmas, and there reflect on what gift we might offer this year and decide how we will live in recognition of our friendship with the creator of the world.

It's very easy, as Christmas fast approaches, to become distracted and suddenly surprised by Christmas itself. With the frenzies of Black Friday and Cyber Monday we can find ourselves swept up in spending. But by offering a gift, you sow a seed that God can grow, to advance His Kingdom. Your heart remains focussed in the direction of Jesus and what you're offering for him.

SCRIPTURE TO CONSIDER: Isa. 7:13–17; Jer. 31:30–34; Matt 6:21; 2 Cor 9:6-8.

AN ACTION TO TAKE: Consider donating to charity today as part of the global day of giving for Giving Tuesday. If you'd like to donate to the work here at Waverley Abbey Trust, you can visit the webite: waverleyabbeyresources. org/make-a-donation

A PRAYER TO MAKE: 'Lord, just as You spoke with Jesus, please speak into my heart and reveal more of Yourself every day. Amen.'

WAVERLEY ABBEY TRUST

One day to
make
a world of
difference

GI♥INGTUESDAY

#GivingTuesday 2021

The global day of generosity takes place TODAY

30 November 2021!

Join thousands of people donating to good causes today.

waverleyabbeyresources.org/make-a-donation

Dear readers,

As we move into December in our time together, we'd like to encourage you to take a look at the Advent resources we've compiled to complement these notes. On our website waverleyabbeyresources.org/advent you'll find information about retreats, special events, resources and further devotional material, all based on the themes we're looking at together in the coming weeks. We'd love you to draw in deeper as we travel together on our Search for God this Christmas time.

Blessings,

Micha Jazz.

John 1:16–9

'In him was life, and that life was the light of all mankind. The light shines in the darkness, and the darkness has not overcome it.' (vv4–5)

Life's a gift! It offers us the chance to go in search of meaning, to make peace with ourselves and life itself. Life offers us options but insight and understanding, come from one enduring origin, God, creator of all. We must find trust in our ability and belief that we can successfully face many daily demands for our confidence to grow. Our capacity for life increases, our judgments improve. Our history impacts us from conception, and we yearn to discover personal security. This lies beyond our natural ability. We can't craft self-esteem from thin air; all we do is put on a mask, and masquerade as someone we aspire to be without realising that aspiration.

This mask is fashioned from our perception of others and our own assumptions. We need an external reference point to understand who and why we are, and to help us find confidence to choose values to live by that will shape our life and relationships.

Jesus is our perpetual life, a lighthouse forever steering us away from the rocks of self-destruction. The whole Christian journey is one of discernment and discovery. First, we discern God's love and then discover we are accepted and loved. Then we begin to discern that we are fearfully and wonderfully made (Psa. 139:14).

No longer are we constrained by our history, nor reduced to masquerading as someone we assume others expect us to be. We find our true identity in friendship with our strongest advocate, God. We switch on the lights and live with confidence in our ability to exercise control over our motivation, behaviour and environment.

SCRIPTURE TO CONSIDER: Psa. 139; Isa. 48:16–22; Rom. 8:1–17; 1 John 1:1–10.

AN ACTION TO TAKE: In a climate that seeks to sell us an identity to mask much of life's pain, take time to consider God's promise of light and life. Need some help? edwj.org/nd21-1dec

A PRAYER TO MAKE: 'Lord, help me to place my complete confidence in You and find my confidence to live every day with Jesus. Amen.'

John 1:6–8

'He came as a witness to testify concerning that light, so that through him all might believe. He Himself was not the light; he came only as a witness to the light.' (vv7–8)

Lighthouses have existed since Egyptian times.* Their purpose is to warn sailors of fatal danger. John the Baptist was a human lighthouse. Confident in his calling he chose a distinct path to express his message preparing people for the ministry of Jesus. He knew his identity and lived his purpose boldly.

Our mortal life acts as a living expression of God's purpose. Just as Jesus became flesh to reveal God's person and purpose (Heb. 1:1-2), so we are to live as witnesses to God's reality.

On our journey to Christmas we are not alone in our search for God. Like John, we've received our commission (Acts 1:8). We are to point in the direction of the babe born in Bethlehem and support people in their search for Jesus.

Interestingly we start right where we are - family, neighbours, colleagues - for this is our Judea. As with everything in life we start in our home and neighbourhood. John witnessed alone, yet we might draw confidence from offering hospitality alongside others. Hence, ensure our church buildings, as well as our houses, have the reputation of providing hospitality. There are so many lonely people in search of a conversation, which affirms their value and establishes a social space in which they can forge friendships. Jesus was the master at initiating conversation with unlikely people (Luke 19:1–5).

SCRIPTURE TO CONSIDER: Isa. 62:1–7; Ezek. 33:1–9; Matt. 3:1–12; Rom. 10:14–20.

AN ACTION TO TAKE: Learn to live as a lighthouse. Begin to offer hospitality and start some conversations within your community.

A PRAYER TO MAKE: 'Lord, just as You are the light of the world, help me to become a bright light for Jesus in my community. Amen.'

* edwj.org/nd21-2dec

Jeremiah 33:12–16

'"The days are coming," declares the LORD, "when I will fulfil the good promise I made to the people of Israel and Judah."' (v14)

Waiting is challenging. Children often find the last few days leading up to Christmas unbearable. They sense the excitement, yet there is nothing they can do to speed its arrival.

Throughout the Old Testament people of faith were invited to wait in expectation for the promised Messiah. Their lives, like ours, were subject to life's ups and downs. In a country squeezed between two world powers (Egypt in the South and then whoever dominated in the North), they faced uncertainty from both the normal storms of life and the terrors of war.

Perhaps, the greatest witness to patient waiting is Job. A man who lost everything precious and lay ill, incapacitated, and had to discover the depth of his confidence in God. Such confidence can only ever be found over a period of time, where uncertainty wrestles with faith as we are tempted to question God's promise of provision for our wilderness experience.

Advent serves as a reminder that immediate gratification may not be our present reality. Living every day with Jesus demands our patience. It's why I consider, at the start of every day, Psalm 46:10: 'Be still, and know that I am God; I will be exalted among the nations, I will be exalted in the earth.'

As we go in search of God, let's be neither discouraged nor despondent at the turns our life takes (Heb. 11:13).

SCRIPTURE TO CONSIDER: Lam. 3:1–33; Isa. 30:15–26; James 5:7–16; Heb. 12:1–13.

AN ACTION TO TAKE: There are times when God invites us to keep going. When the going gets tough, are you able to find the resolve to keep walking with Jesus?

A PRAYER TO MAKE: 'Lord, I am grateful that nothing is impossible with You. May I find my confidence in Your Word every day. Amen.' (Luke 1:37)

Isaiah 6:1–8

'"Woe to me!" I cried. "I am ruined! For I am a man of unclean lips, and I live among a people of unclean lips, and my eyes have seen the King, the LORD Almighty."' (v5)

I f honest, each of us has overreacted to a situation, judged someone unfairly, misinterpreted the tone of an email or social media post, and taken something personally when it wasn't meant that way. The art of pausing and 'counting to ten' has been all but lost as opinions and comments are sprayed like machine gun bullets across the blogosphere.

Isaiah, catching sight of God in all His glory, is reduced to reflecting on his own, miserable self. Any encounter with God reminds us of how small in stature we are compared with God. In acknowledging who he is, Isaiah creates space for God to equip him for who God's ordained him to be. Likewise, we are invited to gaze on God and remind ourselves of our wretched state without God (v5), yet also daring to stand and speak with God in responding to His invitation to serve His purpose on earth (v8).

Integrity begins as we perceive things truly for what they are and set aside all deceits that inevitably obscure both the truth about God and the truth about ourselves from us. It is a moment of relief when we realise God is never disillusioned with us since He never had any illusions to start with (Rom. 5:8). In searching for God, we must first come to terms with the fact that we are nothing without God. Our yearning for God increases exponentially at that point of self-realisation.

SCRIPTURE TO CONSIDER: 2 Chron. 12:6–14; Isa. 64:1–12; Mark 4:9–13; 1 Pet. 2:1–10.

AN ACTION TO TAKE: Compare how you perceive yourself with how others perceive you, after some honest listening? How would you like to be remembered?

A PRAYER TO MAKE: 'Lord, help me to gaze on You and acknowledge my wayward nature, whilst always giving thanks for Your saving grace and call to service. Amen.'

Disagreeing Well

Romans 15:4–13

'May the God who gives endurance and encouragement give you the same attitude of mind toward each other that Christ Jesus had, so that with one mind and one voice you may glorify the God and Father of our Lord Jesus Christ.' (vv5–6)

Many people use an Advent wreath and light a candle for each of the four Sundays leading up to Christmas. The tradition is said to have been recommended by Martin Luther for families to use in their home as they instructed the family on the coming of Christ and encouraged them to live in hope and expectation of His return.*

Others trace its origins to a German pastor Johann Hinrich Wichern (1808-1881) who, in 1829; built a wreath out of an old cartwheel to help the children in his mission school count the days until Christmas.** He added small candles to be lit every weekday and Saturday during Advent and, on Sundays, a large white candle was lit.

We all respond to traditions in different ways. Indeed, we have developed language to describe our different approaches, such as 'high church' and 'low church'. However, God looks not on the outward appearance, but on the heart (1 Sam. 16:7). Just as God unexpectedly chose David as king, so He also accepted his act of repentance after grave sin (2 Sam. 12:7–9).

God challenges us with His invitation to learn to live by faith and not by judgment. Even when we disagree, we are called to pray for those with whom we disagree, not to condemn them (Rom. 12:19).

As we go in search of God, let's search our own hearts and confess to judgments we have made which alone belong to God.

SCRIPTURE TO CONSIDER: Psa. 24; Matt. 7:1–5; 15:1–20; Rom. 2:1–16.

AN ACTION TO TAKE: We are not called to judge on God's behalf (Mark 9:38–41). Enter into conversation and celebrate the shared hope you have, whilst learning to disagree well.

A PRAYER TO MAKE: 'Lord, 'create in me a pure heart' and 'renew a steadfast spirit within me'. Amen.' (Psa. 51:10–11).

* edwj.org/nd21-5dec **The Story of the Advent Wreath, edwj/org/nd21-5dec2

Psalm 43:3–5

'Send me your light and your faithful care, let them lead me; let them bring me to your holy mountain, to the place where you dwell. Then I will go to the altar of God, to God, my joy and my delight. I will praise you with the lyre, O God, my God.' (vv3–4)

Light is 'the natural agent that stimulates sight and makes things visible', something that excites the human visual system.* Without light we cannot see where we're going (Matt. 15:14). We can't find our way since we're consumed in darkness, impotent in determining direction. This is both isolating and frightening. But, in the darkness, we can only await the dawn, a fresh shaft of divine light to lead us on in our walk of faith (Psa. 104:19–23).

Darkness alerts and intensifies our senses, a good reason to consider God's truth. Without light there are fewer distractions, and what engages us is that which might be about to consume us, what we cannot see and also fail to discern.

Israel had been waiting in the dark for four hundred years when Jesus was born. It was a season of expectation following the final prophet Malachi. In Bethlehem, an event that itself lit up the sky for shepherds and wise men alike, a baby was born, one who would excite and stimulate us with a new vision of salvation and recovering our imagination. With light we can travel safely, find our way, always giving thanks to God and going where He leads. We must seek God's light to understand the times in which we live and where we are to invest our energy to serve God's kingdom purpose. Such light lifts our spirit and gives us hope, the true gift of Christmas.

SCRIPTURE TO CONSIDER: Prov. 2:1–15; Matt. 6:19–24; John 9:1–12; 1 John 1:5–10.

AN ACTION TO TAKE: How does God reveal the light of His purpose to you so that you can work it out in your life?

A PRAYER TO MAKE: 'Lord, stimulate my heart and mind with a clear and renewed vision for my life in Your service. Amen.'

* edwj.org/nd21-6dec.

Present Always

Psalm 27:1–4

'Though an army besiege me, my heart will not fear; though war break out against me, even then I will be confident.' (v3)

Recently Jayne woke aware of silent movement in the bedroom. She put on a light to see a bat flying above her. Knowing they navigated by echolocation using ultrasound, she turned off the light and went back to sleep.* The bat was gone by morning.

We need echolocation. God is present throughout history and the only way we can live effectively is to call out and trust God to guide us. Here, the psalmist remains at peace even with the enemy at the gates. God is his, and our, navigator, the light and deliverer from our sin, fear and death – and our salvation. There may be good reasons to fear, but once my understanding is stimulated by the light of God, I grow in confidence despite the evidence before my eyes.

God's presence was once limited to the Temple, now we are all temples of the Holy Spirit (1 Cor. 6:19–20). We abide with God, and God with us, housed within our body. Wherever we go, God is with us. Always accessible, watching over us, observing us, and accessible in every circumstance.

Learning to become conscious of God's continuous presence is one aspect of discipleship, one we can easily neglect. It's the reason we can 'pray continually' (1 Thess. 5:17), for God has brought us to the place where we can 'dwell... gaze... [and] seek him' (Psa. 27:4) every moment of every day.

SCRIPTURE TO CONSIDER: Psa. 139:7–12; Isa. 43:1–8; John 14:15–21; Heb. 4:1–16.

AN ACTION TO TAKE: Take time learning how to become, and remain, conscious of God's presence throughout your day.

A PRAYER TO MAKE: 'Lord, thank You that You are with me every moment of every day throughout my life. Amen.'

* edwj.org/nd21-7dec

Psalm 119:105–112

'Your statutes are my heritage forever; they are the joy of my heart. My heart is set on keeping your decrees to the very end.' (vv111–112)

Heritage lies at the heart of Waverley Abbey. The earliest mention of Farnham is in a 688 charter when Cædwalla, King of Wessex, gave land to two or three monks for a monastery. This became a 'mother' church for the area and recent work has revealed a small church under St Andrew's parish church.*

Today, as I look from the house over to the ruins of the first Cistercian monastery, I'm reminded of the deposit of faith-filled prayer and practice upon which our mission of living every day with Jesus and helping others is built.

St Benedict, in his *Rule* of 516; described monastic life as a school of learning for life. We continue that heritage today with our commitment to encourage people both to discover God for the first time and to deepen their Christian understanding and service.

Everything we have is built on the deposit of faith invested by those who have gone before us. It stands as testimony to our faithful God and a stimulus for each of us to continue to 'run the race' in realising our Christian call (Heb. 12:1).

Scripture is God's story of His faithfulness, as well as His guide to living the God-life today. It's why we encourage everyone to read Scripture daily. For just as our physical bodies need food, so our spirit needs to feed from God's Word. Learning to live God's way is our primary purpose in life.

SCRIPTURE TO CONSIDER: Eccl. 9:11–18; Isa. 40:18–31; 1 Cor. 9:19–27; 2 Tim. 4:1–8.

AN ACTION TO TAKE: Read the stories of women and men of faith who have gone before us and discover how you might invest your life in serving God. Visit edwj.org/nd21-8dec1

A PRAYER TO MAKE: 'Lord, thank You that Your love endures forever. Help me to leave a deposit of faith for future generations. Amen.'

* edwj.org/nd21-8dec

Faith and Doubt

John 12:34–36

'Then Jesus told them, "You are going to have the light just a little while longer. Walk while you have the light, before darkness overtakes you. Whoever walks in the dark does not know where they are going."' (v35)

Christmas celebrates Jesus' birth. But we know His life will end in apparent despair and real desolation. Jesus revealed God's purpose by always doing His Father's bidding (John 5:19). Jesus tells us to obey the Father, with Scripture to guide us. Our challenge? Discerning God's will and purpose.

Fortunately, God doesn't make this difficult. But it demands our time and attention to learn to live God's way. The more we invest in seeking God, the deeper our understanding and confidence will grow.

Our biggest challenge is keeping confidence in God when we lose sight of Him. It becomes difficult when there appears little supporting evidence. Our doubts grow, but these are always legitimate as they test the depth of our real confidence in God.

Doubt is called the shadow of faith. We waver in our conviction. Our problems arise when we choose to live in doubt. We become double-minded and thus unstable, in every area of our life (James 1:8).

Faith is always expressed when we choose to favour God's Word and promise without any evidence to support it (Heb. 11:1). I fell apart caring for my first wife as she struggled with MS. My instability was total. Yet, somehow I clung to God's promise and my faith survived and deepened. Being real and struggling are legitimate expressions of our walk of faith. Let's be kind to ourselves and others in times of darkness.

SCRIPTURE TO CONSIDER: Prov. 3:1–8; Matt. 14:22–33; Mark 9:14–24; Heb. 11:1–40.

AN ACTION TO TAKE: Where are you struggling between faith and doubt? This is not sin; it's the challenge of the Christian life. Pray and seek the encouragement and support of Christian friends.

A PRAYER TO MAKE: 'Lord, I believe and I struggle. Help me to hold on to faith, even when I cannot see the answers to my prayers. Amen.'

Ephesians 5:3–13

**'Let no one deceive you with empty words, for because of
such things God's wrath comes on those who are disobedient.
Therefore do not be partners with them.'** (vv6–7)

The Bible sets high standards (vv3–4). I've spoken empty words far
too often. Knowing where my mind has taken me, and where I've
let myself down under peer pressure and personal preference, it is
grace alone on which I remain totally dependent.

It is impossible to live the Christian life by force of will. To do so is to
draw on my own strength, the very opposite of what Jesus instructs us
to do in trusting Him (Mark 5:36). Christianity is not an outward mask,
but an inner conviction. Yes, it can and will produce changes, but it also
invites us to become aware of our corruption (1 Cor. 15:42–44).

Sanctification is a painful process. As I draw nearer to God, I become
increasingly aware of my mortal corruption. With the best will in the
world I cannot please God, but can accept His generous gift of grace,
acceptance and salvation.

Then I choose the degree to which I want to develop that friendship
with God. In the myriad opportunities that life affords, where will I
invest my time and energy? I only began heavily investing in God from
my mid-forties. Up to then, although a Christian in ministry, I played
far too fast and loose with God's kindness. Now I am conscious how
'the things of earth' grow 'strangely dim in the light of [God's] glory and
grace'.* A song I sang so often as a young Christian is now my heart's
deep desire, and my life's refrain.

SCRIPTURE TO CONSIDER: Gen. 50:15–26; Ezek. 36:33–38; Matt. 10:26–33; Eph.
4:1–16.

AN ACTION TO TAKE: When we fail, it's an opportunity to return to God's grace to
request and receive God's forgiveness. Do you want to live by and grow in
God's grace?

A PRAYER TO MAKE: 'Lord, when I'm weary and troubled and can see no light in
the darkness, may I embrace Your grace. Amen.'

*Turn Your Eyes upon Jesus by Helen H. Lemmel, 1922: edwj.org/nd21-10dec [accessed 24/07/2021]

1 Peter 2:2–10

'You also, like living stones, are being built into a spiritual house to be a holy priesthood, offering spiritual sacrifices acceptable to God through Jesus Christ.' (v5)

Last August we opened Waverley Abbey's Café at weekends. It was wonderful to welcome our local Farnham neighbours, and others, to enjoy the hospitality and renewal the House and Abbey afford.

One visitor I spoke to remembered with joy reading *EDWJ* and purchasing a brick to enable Selwyn Hughes to buy the House in the 1980s. It reminded me, and still does, that all those who purchased a brick invested prayerfully and financially in seeding a vision that still deepens faith and trains people for acts of service. This work of building a spiritual house is to empower and equip people, yet also to ensure there is a holy space in which learning can take place, welcome and hospitality is offered, and wisdom shared, all arising from continuous prayer.

Selwyn cast a vision for Waverley university, one that would train 'people helpers', who in turn could realise Jesus' commission to travel to 'the ends of the earth' (Acts 1:8). We continue that work of together, today, and in reality are simply the living stones who, with those who have preceded us, will become God's means for realising this essential vision.

We are chosen by God and invited to serve His purpose through our lives. The history of mission is the work of faithful people, freed by God's Spirit, to dream and invest everything they are and have into developing a vision that will best serve future generations. Waverley Abbey University is one such vision; join your prayers with ours in this work of God.

SCRIPTURE TO CONSIDER: Neh. 1:1–11; Isa. 65:1–10; Mark 10:35–45; Gal. 6:1–10.

AN ACTION TO TAKE: Find out more about how Selwyn's vision for a Christian university continues to take shape. How might you help the fulfilment of this vision? edwj.org/nd21-11dec

A PRAYER TO MAKE: 'Lord, my heart and my desire is to see Your vision realised. May I, as a living stone, ensure I am in the right place for serving You every day. Amen.'

Isaiah 60:1–4
**'Arise, shine, for your light has come, and the
glory of the LORD rises upon you.'** (v1)

Observing sunrises is associated with summer, not winter. Yet they still occur. Waiting for sunrise takes patience. Once, on the slopes of Mt Subasio above Assisi, Italy, I waited to see the sun rise above the Apennines. It was cold and took time as light quietly preceded the bright orb's return.

Shadow made way for the dawn, before shafts of sunlight started kissing the landscape. Then we were finally embraced within its warmth. Like our search for God, there are many signs of God's presence before we enter His reality. Indeed, the joy of our life journey is that we daily discover more of God's presence before finally experiencing the dawning of our perpetual rest in God's presence.

On Subasio that morning, some chose not to join us, preferring sleep. In doing so, whilst they later rejoined us, they had not shared an encounter with the dawn. So, we need to be awake to the opportunity to know God continuously. One reason I pray and read Scripture on waking is to begin my day as I intend to live it (Psa. 108:1–2).

Life's responsibilities and pressures can dumb our sense of God's presence. These wrestle to assert themselves as the dominant theme of our existence, and despondency easily casts its long shadow across our spirit. Here, we must wake up and join with creation to declare the glory of the Lord (Psa.19:1).

SCRIPTURE TO CONSIDER: Psa. 95; 103:1–5; Isa. 40:21–26; Luke 1:46–56.

AN ACTION TO TAKE: When you feel the shadows of despondency creeping up on you, what is your response? Seek to look for the warmth of God's love and acceptance, the sign of God's presence.

A PRAYER TO MAKE: 'Lord, may the dawning of Your love embrace me every day, dispersing the shadows of despondency. Amen.'

2 Corinthians 4:1–6

'The god of this age has blinded the minds of unbelievers, so that they cannot see the light of the gospel that displays the glory of Christ, who is the image of God.' (v4)

The best of intentions is subject to sabotage, often by our own hand. Simply responding to Jesus is a great first step into a life subject to constant change – but only ever a first step.

We are all used to seeing bright sunshine suddenly obscured by passing clouds. So with us. We feel full of God's Spirit and then darkness engulfs us, we struggle and fall. This is the nature of growing into maturity in Christ. The perennial question remains; how much do we want Jesus?

The god of this age hasn't taken a holiday since the terminal setback of Christ's resurrection. He's a stalker, and we are the prey (1 Pet. 5:8–9). So there are times when God tests our resolve to follow and our capacity to love and trust God. This builds spiritual resilience and adaptation. We are to work at building this as we go in search of our God of glory. We walk along many valleys beneath the shadow of death and, although intimidated, we must choose to fight for and lay hold of all we need from God. Resisting wrongdoing, and deliberately saying yes to God, we can adopt a new song affirming our confidence in God; 'You are the way when there seems to be no way, we trust in You, God, You alone have the final say'.*

SCRIPTURE TO CONSIDER: Ezek. 37:1–14; Rom. 7:7–8:4; 2 Cor. 4:7–18; Rev. 3:14–22.

AN ACTION TO TAKE: Life is demanding and subject to setbacks that shake us to our core. We are to look to God who told us to pray and mountains will move (Mark 11:22–25). Are you ready to enrol in the school that teaches mountain moving?

A PRAYER TO MAKE: 'Lord, bright as the morning star. Jesus, how can I tell You how beautiful You are to me? Jesus, song that the angels sing. Jesus, dearer to my heart than anything.' I surrender afresh to Your love today. Amen.'**

Believe For It by CeCe Winans (FRTS © 2021): edwj.org/nd21-13dec
**Jesus You're Beautiful* by CeCe Winans. Lyrics by Sabin Nathan Orville (Pure Springs Music © 2003)

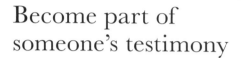

Become part of someone's testimony

Our Bible reading notes are read by hundreds of thousands of people around the world, and *Every Day with Jesus* and *Inspiring Women Every Day* have recently been made free in the UK. We want everyone, whatever their financial means, to have access to these resources that help them walk each day with our Saviour.

Here's what one Every Day with Jesus reader wrote to us:

Ever since I started using Everyday with Jesus, I reconnected to the Lord directly again. It deals with my day to day and minute to minute problems in details. Guiding me in the most solemn and right direction for a dedicated Christian living.

As we trust in God's provision, we know there are costs to providing this ministry. Do you have a passion for God's Word changing lives? Could supporting this vision be a way in which you serve?

A gift of just £2 a month from you will put daily Bible reading notes into the hands of at least one person who is hungry to know God and experience His presence every day.

Visit **waverleyabbeyresources.org/donate** to become part of someone's testimony, or use the form at the back of these notes.

1 John 1:4–10

'If we claim to have fellowship with him and yet walk in the darkness, we lie and do not live out the truth. But if we walk in the light, as he is in the light, we have fellowship with one another, and the blood of Jesus, his Son, purifies us from all sin.' (vv6–7)

Many never find the fullness of God they yearn for. That is because we live between the devil's darkness and the light of God. Our society places huge pressure upon us to conform to standards that are irrelevant as far as the gospel is concerned.

The Mosaic Code presented behavioural standards, but life with Christ is relational and not a performance. However, often we feel there's a standard to maintain. Church can become an insincere context where we wear metaphorical masks, fearing our true life will be exposed, judged and rejected.

There is a price to pay for transparency, for when we discover we can live by God's Word through His Spirit we threaten the very edifice of social constructs, in choosing not to pursue money, sex and power. Although not intrinsically wrong, being sacred gifts from God, He urges us to live appropriately in respect to them since they have a powerful capacity to corrupt our lives.*The disciple declares active war on everything that undermines God's complete authority in our lives. The escape route is to kneel before God, confess weakness with honesty and to walk away from the compromises money, sex and power will always demand in our witness and service of God. Listen to God. He knows our weaknesses and has provided each of us with a guaranteed way of escape (1 Cor. 10:13).

SCRIPTURE TO CONSIDER: Prov. 4:18–27; Isa. 42:10–25; Eph. 5:8–20; Rom. 11:11–14.

AN ACTION TO TAKE: Get hold of a copy of Richard Foster's *Money, Sex & Power* from edwj.org/nd21-14dec

A PRAYER TO MAKE: 'Lord, keep encouraging me to have the courage to live a transparent life in the light, and avoid the darkness that surrounds me. Amen.'

*Richard Foster, *Money, Sex & Power*

John 3:16–21
'Whoever believes in him is not condemned, but whoever does not believe stands condemned already because they have not believed in the name of God's one and only Son.' (v18)

It's sometimes difficult to believe, when all the evidence suggests that all we are believing in is disintegrating before our very eyes. Each of us will have a story where, when invited to believe, we stumbled and messed up.

God doesn't condemn us when we are seeking to believe but we run out of faith along the way. Questions pop up and we have to pause, reflect and make up our mind if we will believe or walk away disappointed.

Belief is to place our full confidence in God. Confidence simply means 'firmly trusting'.* We've already noted that doubt accompanies faith – so we hold on by our fingertips. The Christian path is not necessarily easy, but it is simple.

It's a lot easier to ditch God than hold on through the night, patiently waiting for dawn to break. There's no hiding from the fact that belief will demand all we have. Belief is an act of the will when reason and emotion yell their complaint and demand our surrender. But, if we will hold our ground, in time we will see the working of God's purpose through our lives.

The Christian message is simply a conviction that, despite evidence to the contrary, God is present, always in charge and will sustain us. Darkness, believing that life is a roulette wheel based on chance, may be easier to live with, yet offers us no greater assurance than believing in God's promise. *etymonline.com description of 'confidence

---

SCRIPTURE TO CONSIDER: Psa. 16; Lam. 3:1–33; Rom. 5:1–11; James 1:2–18.

AN ACTION TO TAKE: How much confidence do you have in God when prayers appear unanswered and outcomes are far from what you wanted or anticipated?

A PRAYER TO MAKE: 'Lord, I believe; help my unbelief (Mark 9:24). Enable me to keep faith in You through the darkness. Amen.'

Isaiah 40:1–11

'Speak tenderly to Jerusalem, and proclaim to her that her hard service has been completed, that her sin has been paid for, that she has received from the LORD's hand double for all her sins.' (v2)

Bound by the limitations of mortality, we can't fully grasp God's perspective. We think in weeks; God holds *eternity* in His hands (Isa. 43:11–13). At both the beginning and the end, He perpetually sees the substance of everything. Following God requires our trust, especially when life makes no immediate sense.

Yet, God understands our pain and lives within the questions we carry. For if I were able to access answers to all my questions, I'd enjoy access to aspects of God that lie far beyond human wisdom.

However, God is our shepherd (v11) and sustains us even as we struggle with making sense of life. Let's be kind to ourselves and each other as we face the uncertainties life places along the way. At the incarnation Jesus emptied Himself and chose to live among us, to remove the separation existing between us and God.

This is our source of hope on which we focus, travelling through treacherous landscapes. Remarkably, we are invited to rest in God with confidence when we appear to have lost our footing, for God alone knows what tomorrow brings. When we think about it, our mind is besieged by the worst of our imaginings and God's promise can sink beneath the depths of our despondent mood. We choose to pause and 'see, the Sovereign LORD comes with power, and... rules with a mighty arm ... his reward is with him, and his recompense accompanies him' (v10).

SCRIPTURE TO CONSIDER: Deut. 31:1–13; John 10:1–18; Heb. 13:1–19; Rev. 22:12–21.

AN ACTION TO TAKE: When life is difficult, focus on the promise that God is with you and knows the end from the beginning. Get a copy of *Your Personal Encourager* to strengthen your faith edwj.org/nd21-16dec

A PRAYER TO MAKE: 'Lord, as my good shepherd, please guide and sustain me each and every day in whatever I encounter in my life. Amen.'

Personal Responsibility **FRIDAY 17 DECEMBER**

John 9:1–11

**'After saying this, he spat on the ground, made some mud
with the saliva, and put it on the man's eyes. "Go," he told
him, "wash in the Pool of Siloam" (this word means "Sent"). So
the man went and washed, and came home seeing.'** (vv6–7)

As Christians, we enter into a partnership with God, which operates
when we choose to obey and do as God directs. Here, the blind
man discovers three things, still relevant today.

He learns that sin is not the source of sickness (v3). We are invited
to discover the grace and goodness of God in all aspects of life. This
challenges many of the frames of reference we have adopted from our
upbringing, education and assumptions about life. This is testing but
offers one measure of the sincerity of our faith.

The next lesson is that God holds in His hands the true purpose
of our life. This season on earth is not our destination, rather an
opportunity to live as a witness to our creator and the kingdom that
remains His to reveal. One day we shall leave this mortal sphere and
live for ever in the very presence of God. Mortality brings with it pain
and challenge; can we trust God's overarching purpose within it?

Finally, having encountered God, the man must respond and obey
God's instruction. It is perhaps an unusual method of healing, but he
wants his sight and so enters the Pool of Siloam, built by a king who
also experienced a miraculous healing (2 Kings 20:20). Whilst his sight
returns, the critical sign is that God brings light to the darkness that
surrounds us all – for God is light eternal – revealing the way we can
discover fullness of life.

SCRIPTURE TO CONSIDER: Psa. 138; Eccl. 12:9–14; Matt. 16:24–27; 2 Cor. 12:5–10.

AN ACTION TO TAKE: How can you build an effective partnership with God, where
your life and experience offers God the opportunity to reveal His kingdom
today?

A PRAYER TO MAKE: 'Lord, help me daily to live out Your purpose through my life
and bring glory to You. Amen.'

Luke 3:1–6

'A voice of one calling in the wilderness, "Prepare the way for the Lord, make straight paths for him. Every valley shall be filled in, every mountain and hill made low. The crooked roads shall become straight, the rough ways smooth. And all people will see God's salvation."' (vv4b–6)

Christianity is rooted in biblical revelation. This collection of scriptures provides our understanding of how God works in a world consumed by its own pursuit of truth. Such is humanity's presumption that it believes it has the competence to understand the origins of life. Yet, whilst answers are presented, they lead to many more questions.

The incarnation marks God's intervention, a central aspect of a plan long prepared (Rom. 5:6). A whole series of events, designed within the heart of God, were set in motion. The miraculous conception of Jesus' cousin John (known as 'the Baptist') provided a voice calling people back to repentance. Four hundred years of silence were shattered by that voice calling people in the wilderness of their personal emptiness.

Where there is no voice, no one can find Jesus' message of salvation. Each of us has a story of God's work in our life. Let's raise our voices to share the power of personal testimony. It offers the unanswerable argument for God's grace, describing how God makes sense in the particulars of our life. It speaks of our confidence in God, the substance of where valleys have been filled and mountains flattened.

Our story is so important because it tells us, and assures others, of the practical application of God's truth; we are the Bible in action.

SCRIPTURE TO CONSIDER: Isa. 45:1–13; Mal. 3:1–5; Matt. 11:1–14; John 15:18–27.

AN ACTION TO TAKE: Take time to reflect on where God is at work in your own life. With whom can you share your story?

A PRAYER TO MAKE: 'Lord, my road is long and there are mountains in my way. Help me climb a step each and every day. Amen.'*

*From *Up Where We Belong,* by Jack Nitzsche, Buffy Sainte-Marie and Will Jennings. (Sony/ATV Music Publishing LLC © 1982)

Isaiah 11:1–9
**'He will not judge by what he sees with his eyes, or decide
by what he hears with his ears; but with righteousness
he will judge the needy, with justice he will give
decisions for the poor of the earth.'** (vv3b–4a)

One week to Christmas Day. For those lighting candles in their Advent wreath, today's candle traditionally represents peace. Our world is always in need of peace, and of course one of Jesus' titles is Prince of Peace (Isa. 9:6)

For peace to preside, there must be some authority to establish order, and Jesus is that supreme authority. Present at the creation of the universe, He knows how all things hold together (Col. 1:17). Yet, we know from Genesis that we play our part in sustaining that peace. God never enforces His authority but invites us to implement it through our actions. When we fail then there is a breakdown of the order within God's kingdom and space is created for effective enemy action (Gen. 3:21–24).

Jesus' incarnation is the budding of God's purpose in restoring relationship with humanity. Years of waiting and calling out to God begin to bear the early signs of harvest. It's a reminder that our times are in God's hands (Psa. 31:14–15a). It's why we celebrate Christmas, the reopening of a long-lost door into God's welcome acceptance and embrace.

It's little wonder that the beneficial reason for Christmas can so easily be lost in the cacophony of misplaced celebration. We enjoy the apparent peace afforded by a long Christmas break, yet sadly a peace without order, a peace that quickly disintegrates based only on empty longing. Ensure Jesus is the centre of your Christmas this year.

SCRIPTURE TO CONSIDER: Psa. 119:161–168; Isa. 26:1–6; Matt. 5:1–12; Rom. 12:9–21.

AN ACTION TO TAKE: Look over the statements in the Matthew selection. How might you implement these in your daily life?

A PRAYER TO MAKE: 'Lord, encourage me to hate what is evil and love what is good. Amen.'

Zephaniah 3:14–17
**'The LORD has taken away your punishment, he has
turned back your enemy. The LORD, the King of Israel, is
with you; never again will you fear any harm.'** (v15)

The Christian life is counter-intuitive. We are taught from birth to do
all we might to avoid pain – physical, emotional and psychological.
I was naive enough once to think I could live just such a life. Even
after finding faith and accepting that to andbad things happen to God's
good people, I wanted to assume that God would spare me. And of
course He didn't.

In the fury of the storm that engulfed me I quickly appreciated how
little time I had invested in laying solid foundations for my faith. I truly
was like a ship without a rudder, tossed to and fro upon the roughest
of seas. On reflection, I inwardly groan at the degree to which my
Christian façade collapsed, established as it was on the quicksand
of ego, pride and wishful thinking. I wondered if there was anything
substantial about my faith, or was I simply one of the hypocrites who
talked a good game?

It was in learning to trust in both the truth and power of God's Word
that began a process of rebuilding. Like Francis of Assisi, I had to go
in search of bricks and slowly attempt to repair this temple of the Holy
Spirit now devastated by forces of nature well beyond my control.

Since then I have made some progress, further storms have come
and gone and, despite some necessary repairs, the temple has stood
firm. I no longer fear harm, I've found my faith legs, I will entrust myself
to God in any storm.

SCRIPTURE TO CONSIDER: Psa. 42; Micah 7:1–7; Matt. 7:24–29; 2 Cor. 1:3–11.

AN ACTION TO TAKE: It's only by working our faith muscle that we can be sure of
withstanding the storm. That's the primary reason we seek to learn to live
every day with Jesus.

A PRAYER TO MAKE: 'Lord, may I grow like a tree planted by water, that 'yields its
fruit in season', 'whose leaf does not wither' and learns to prosper in Your
love alone. Amen.' (see Psa. 1:1–6)

Matthew 1:18–25

'Because Joseph her husband was faithful to the law, and yet did not want to expose her to public disgrace, he had in mind to divorce her quietly. But after he had considered this, an angel of the Lord appeared to him in a dream' (vv19–20a)

Christmas is a season of wonder. The incarnation is surrounded with mystery as God breaks in. How completely we take the Gospel reports seriously may well depend on our appetite for the supernatural. But for me this is pure history!

I am in awe of a teenager who accepts the invitation of an angel to carry the Son of God. Without hesitation, Mary was willing to face public disgrace and personal exclusion, if not death. Naivety or faith? I think it is simply the courage and optimism of youth. Something our dour world could do with a strong dose of. Let's encourage a rising generation to take their place in leading God's purpose around the globe.

Then there's Joseph. Apparently betrayed, for betrothal was akin to marriage in his society. Yet, he was not prepared to subject his fiancée to public shame; perhaps one reason God chose these two to usher in the new age of God's kingdom.

In an age of reason, it's easy to lose sight of the miraculous – but we do so at our peril. If we can no longer believe in a God who can suspend the laws of nature at will, then we worship a false god. I would encourage us to read the miraculous narrative of that first Christmas, together with the prophecies that foretold it, and call out to God for miracles in our contemporary world. Not for our benefit – that's selfishness – but for the needs of a distressed world, down the road or on the other side of the world.

SCRIPTURE TO CONSIDER: 2 Kings 4:38–43; Jer. 32:16–27; Mark 10:17–31; Acts 22:1–21.

AN ACTION TO TAKE: Do you struggle with the thought of a supernatural God? Read the Bible and count the miracles that declare the Mystery, our God.

A PRAYER TO MAKE: 'Lord, awaken the faith that enabled Mary and Joseph to say yes to an angel and change the course of history for all. Amen.'

Luke 2:8–21
**'But Mary treasured up all these things and
pondered them in her heart.'** (v19)

If we treasure something, we store it up for future use. The UK Treasury maintains the economy, promoting conditions that enable economic growth and stability at home and abroad. The kingdom of God offers a treasury of wisdom, which is the currency, and ensures its effective growth.

Mary reached full-term, and her child awakened the world to a new age. This was one in which God chose to make Himself available in friendship to every mortal. Shepherds, whose witness society would not accept in court because it was regarded as untrustworthy, were entrusted by God with the first announcement of Jesus' birth. God's economy invites and welcomes the margins into the centre (Luke 4: 18–20). No matter our history or background, God sees the divine spark within each one of us. God refuses to judge us on our past, but on the basis of our response to His invitation of salvation. And, like the shepherds, encounter with God turns our curses to praise and drives us to our knees in grateful worship.

Whilst the shepherds testified to all they had seen and experienced, Mary quietly stored all she observed in the treasury of her heart. It would become the resource she would need throughout a life of loving and serving her Son, Jesus.

This Christmas may be the time to open an account in the bank of Jesus, where the currency is the wisdom needed to live a life of purpose whilst experiencing hope for your future. Or it might afford the opportunity for some healthy auditing of your current savings.

SCRIPTURE TO CONSIDER: Psa. 90:10–17; 1 Cor. 3:10–23; James 1:5–18.

AN ACTION TO TAKE: Use Christmas to review the state of your heart's savings. Is there a rich deposit of wisdom, or is the vault empty? As the shepherds did, make your way to Jesus and reinstate your account.

A PRAYER TO MAKE: 'Lord, like Mary may I take time to store up wisdom in my heart and draw from this in the challenges I face in my daily life. Amen.'

John 12:35–46
'Then Jesus told them, "You are going to have the light just a little while longer. Walk while you have the light, before darkness overtakes you. Whoever walks in the dark does not know where they are going."' (v35)

Christmas is a season of light, from Christmas trees to gaudy house extravaganzas. These all symbolise Jesus, the light of the world, arriving with the gospel message that sin is defeated and we are free to follow and worship God.

However, the invitation is not one we can ignore. Too often we push it to the back of our mind and concentrate on other interests in life. Yet, as with every invitation there is an expiry date. Once that day arrives, we are plunged back into darkness and, with the best will in the world, discovering Jesus afresh becomes very difficult.

Jesus' simple invitation was, 'follow me', which the first disciples accepted as their heart response at the moment of its utterance (Luke 5:27–28). We cannot delay because we don't know what tomorrow might bring. We all have experience of just how suddenly our world gets turned upside down. Only God can return it right side up.

So don't delay. Always follow the intuition of your heart when it comes to Jesus, who is forever seeking to remain in conversation with you. Too often we are more afraid of what it might mean within our existing network of relationships. Well, it takes courage to follow Jesus; yet as people found in Jesus' day, many who wanted to follow Jesus found that they 'loved human praise more than praise from God' (v43). Yet human praise fades on the lips that speak it, whilst God's praise resonates forever.

SCRIPTURE TO CONSIDER: Isa. 54:1–8; John 1:43–51; Rom. 2:12–29; 1 Cor 4:1–13.

AN ACTION TO TAKE: Find a moment on Christmas Day to commit your life once again to the light of the world, Jesus? Life is found in Jesus and Him alone.

A PRAYER TO MAKE: 'Lord, help me to walk in the way of Your truth, 'my soul yearns for you in the night; and in the morning my spirit longs for you'. Amen.' (from Isa. 26:7–9)

Ephesians 1:11–14

'And you also were included in Christ when you heard the message of truth, the gospel of your salvation. When you believed, you were marked in him with a seal, the promised Holy Spirit' (v13)

The seal of the Holy Spirit is like an engagement ring. It demonstrates that we are pledged to God, and shall ultimately be a part of the mysterious Bride of Christ (2 Cor. 11:2–3). We are joined to Christ 'the hour we first believed'. Christmas is God's proposal to humanity. We receive an invitation to share our life entirely with God. As in every engagement there are ups and downs. However, we do all the falling out, for God is constant and true to His promises.

Relationships are the product of many decisions. Separation, created by what appears legitimate anger in the moment of its explosive outburst, can only be recovered through eating humble pie and apologising. So, with God, we find ourselves stepping in and out of God's embrace like a yo-yo. Only as we settle and decide to commit entirely to the relationship as valuable in itself, can we find the resilience to press on deeper into God's heart.

Tantrums laid aside, we discover a rich repository of life, love, acceptance and joy. This despite the tears that mark our cheeks with the sadness that inevitably shapes our life's narrative. There's an advertising slogan, 'A puppy's for life, not just for Christmas'; this applies so much more to the greatest Christmas gift, Jesus Christ, 'love divine, all love excelling'.**

SCRIPTURE TO CONSIDER: Song of Songs 8:5–14; Isa. 62:1–7; John 3:27–36; Rev. 19:1–10.

AN ACTION TO TAKE: Keeping faith with God is to commit to building an exclusive relationship with Jesus through the Spirit. Are you willing to keep faith with your commitment to Christ?

A PRAYER TO MAKE: 'Lord, may I always keep my eyes focused on You and take the time to nurture and nourish the gift of my engagement to You. Amen.'

**Love Divine* by Charles Wesley: edwj.org/nd21-24dec1 [accessed 12/08/2021]

Luke 1:39–56

'From now on all generations will call me blessed, for the Mighty One has done great things for me – holy is his name. His mercy extends to those who fear him, from generation to generation.' (vv48b–50)

Happy Christmas! The rush towards Christmas has ended. We awake to the hushed silence of the feast of Christ's birth. What's true of our physical experience is also true for our spirit.

Mary, after all the shocking events of Gabriel's annunciation, 'hurried' to visit her cousin Elizabeth (v39). Looking for reassurance for the bold 'yes' she has given to God, He confirms His word at the first greeting between the two women. Elizabeth prophesies over Mary and Mary responds, singing God's promise.

Christmas is about our encounter with God. It's easy to fall into a habit of treating it as an observance, of following a religious custom; all activity, no substance. Christmas sweeps past us with a flurry of celebration, with little or no room left for Jesus. I understand the challenge. With our daughter, Christmas Day began with a birthday cake and candles; with us singing happy birthday to Jesus together. We wanted her to know whose day this was, and she loves cakes and candles. Mary declares that the impact of this first Christmas will resonate throughout history until Christ returns. What song will we sing this Christmas, what gifts will we present before Christ's throne (Heb. 4:16)? The physical silence that marks the start of our Christmas offers a moment to pause and surrender once more, as Mary did, to the priority of God's purpose in our life.

SCRIPTURE TO CONSIDER: Isa. 9:1–7; Luke 1:26–38,57–80; Eph. 2:11–22.

AN ACTION TO TAKE: What will you bring to Jesus this Christmas? Find your voice and sing an anthem of praise and promise from your heart.

A PRAYER TO MAKE: 'Lord, my soul glorifies You, 'and my spirit rejoices in God my Saviour' (see vv46-47). I am grateful that You continue to be mindful of me every day. Amen.'

Freely Give

Psalm 108:1–5

'I will praise you, LORD, among the nations; I will sing of you among the peoples. For great is your love, higher than the heavens; your faithfulness reaches to the skies.' (vv3–4)

In Britain, December 26 is a public holiday called Boxing Day. Established in the nineteenth century, servants were given the day off and the wealthy provided boxes of food for poor people. Traditionally in England we go for a long walk, graze off the cold cuts from Christmas leftovers, and generally wind down. It's a day of reflection after the energetic fun and frivolity of the previous day. It always feels as if there is space, and it is wonderful to wake up knowing there is nothing that must be done today.

It is a day for celebrating the love of God, expressed in the gift of Jesus; to acknowledge our salvation freely given; to consider our rich Christian heritage and all that God has done, and continues to do, for us through His boundless love (Eph. 3:20).

I also want to recommend that we take a moment to consider how we might respond to God. It is our ministry here at Waverley Abbey to encourage people to engage with the Bible and learn to live every day with Jesus, so that they might themselves help others. It is our commitment to make these notes as widely available as possible, expanding their distribution throughout the UK and around the world to encourage Christian discipleship and introduce people to God's love.

Will you join me in making a donation, our 'boxed gift', to ensure those without the sustenance of God's Word might enjoy access to this bread of life in this next year?

SCRIPTURE TO CONSIDER: Prov. 11:23–31; Mal. 3:8–12; 2 Cor. 9:6–15; Eph. 3:14–19.

AN ACTION TO TAKE: If you want to join me in making a gift to Waverley Abbey's ministry to make God known through God's Word, then please make your donation at edwj.org/nd21-26dec1

A PRAYER TO MAKE: 'Lord, help me to sow seed faithfully and may it yield a hundredfold return to the glory of Your name. Amen.' (Mark 4:20)

* edwj.org/nd21-26dec2

God's Word, God's Will and God's Work

In the next issue of EDWJ we shall look at God's Word, God's Will, and God's Work.

As Joshua was commanded to keep God's Word always on his lips (V8), so our lives must be deeply rooted in God's Word. Our lives can then draw from God's Truth, like a tree planted by streams of water (Ps. 1:3). We may then discover God's will for our lives and so fulfil God's work.

This is the way God equips and enables us to, `become mature, attaining to the whole measure of the fullness of Christ' (Eph:4:13b).

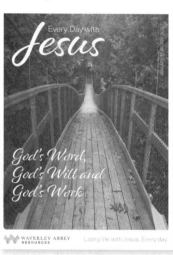

Also available as esubscription, ebook, audioversion and PDF.

Let's Go

Luke 2:13–15

'When the angels had left them and gone into heaven, the shepherds said to one another, "Let's go to Bethlehem and see this thing that has happened, which the Lord has told us about."' (v15)

God speaks to provoke a response. He is never static. We live in an age where the goal is the accumulation of knowledge, but knowledge is there to enable us to perform better in life. So, all that we observe, encounter and mentally absorb is meant to find expression through our lives.

Social media creates armchair commentators. No one examines credentials for those making their statements, but by 'liking' what they say we propel personal opinions to universal significance. Jesus was born before the world was networked. Yet, His birth in a cattle shed in the middle of nowhere laid the foundation for a global awakening. God certainly announced the arrival of Jesus with a full concert of angels but their audience, the shepherds, was small and was left to choose how to respond.

Jesus always wants to shake us out of our lethargy and take who we are and what we have in our hands and put us to work with purpose in His kingdom. First, the shepherds had to find Jesus, then they started telling their story to whoever they met (Luke 2:20).

So today, let's invite God to shake us out of our lethargy. Let's respond by deliberately returning to Christ's crib, discarding the wrapping paper, rich food and drink, and start to tell the story of Jesus' impact and influence on our lives once more. Let's consider how we can invest both who we are and what we have to hand in serving God first and foremost in this year ahead.

SCRIPTURE TO CONSIDER: Psa. 65; Jer. 31:27–34; Heb. 10:19–39; James 1:19–27.

AN ACTION TO TAKE: Ensure you find some time to step aside and kneel before Christ's crib today. What can you commit to God today?

A PRAYER TO MAKE: 'Lord, we glorify and praise You for all the things we have heard and seen, which are just as they have been told in Your Word. Amen.' (Luke 2:20)

Luke 2:28–35

'For my eyes have seen your salvation, which you have prepared in the sight of all nations: a light for revelation to the Gentiles, and the glory of your people Israel.' (vv30–32)

Forty days after Jesus' birth, Mary presented herself with her Son for purification to fulfil Mosaic Law. Here Simeon took Jesus in his arms and prophesied the heart of the Christmas message for all time. It is hard to wait for God's moments that we've already perceived in the eyes of God's Spirit, but not yet manifested on earth. Israel had lived in prophetic silence for four hundred years for the Messiah. Simeon can't contain his excitement. He announces that salvation, through Christ, is for everyone, both Jew and Gentile, confirming this is the Messiah.

The wonder of the Christmas message of God's rescue is that it is available now to anyone who wants to take up God's promise. Only those who freely choose to exclude themselves remain outside its provisions.

However, blessing comes with consequences. In accepting God's gift of salvation, we are invited not simply to give thanks and move on but to embrace the way of life that Jesus modelled through His later ministry.

His own mother heard from Simeon's lips that, whilst her child was the Saviour of the world, this could only come at the cost of His life and the consequential pain of watching her Son be crucified (vv34–35). The walk of faith always involves much waiting, challenging choices and painful experiences, but these ensure the availability of the Christmas message of hope and welcome to all.

SCRIPTURE TO CONSIDER: Psa. 148; Isa. 61:10–62:3; Acts 7:51–60; Gal. 4:4–11.

AN ACTION TO TAKE: Are there promises that you are holding onto by faith? Renew your confidence in waiting and praying for their realisation.

A PRAYER TO MAKE: 'Lord, thank You for rescuing me. Help me to wait patiently, choose wisely and live courageously. Amen.'

Isaiah 49:5–7

'He says: "It is too small a thing for you to be my servant to restore the tribes of Jacob and bring back those of Israel I have kept. I will also make you a light for the Gentiles, that my salvation may reach to the ends of the earth."' (v6)

Christianity is born out of hospitality, which means 'friendliness to guests'.* And everyone living on God's earth is a guest. As Christ's disciples, we are invited by Jesus to offer the gift of friendliness.

Not all of us feel comfortable in a social setting. It's one reason God creates His family, often expressed through church congregations. Yet, the Church's primary purpose is to reflect the present reality of Jesus. Too often it becomes introverted and consumed with its own existence. The Church does not exist to facilitate church.

We know that the church is not its furnishings but its people. Piles of stones cemented into a symbol of religion mark the landscape, yet can only ever offer physical shelter from the rain. As God's living stones, we enjoy the challenge and opportunity to welcome, feed, encourage and be friends with anyone looking for some company. Loneliness is on the rise. In England alone, twenty-five million people report feeling lonely 'occasionally, sometimes or often'.** The shepherds responded to their personal invitation to visit Jesus. We can also extend an invitation to people to come and hang out with us, not for our formal meetings, but to enjoy coffee, cake and conversation. Mission is so fun!

Hospitality lies at the heart of our mission and ministry at Waverley Abbey. Make it yours too in this year ahead.

SCRIPTURE TO CONSIDER: Matt. 25:34–40; Luke 14:12–14; Heb. 13:1–3; 1 Pet. 2:4–12.

AN ACTION TO TAKE: Hospitality is offering the gift of friendliness to people. How can you and your church be more hospitable within your community?

A PRAYER TO MAKE: 'Lord, I am grateful knowing that I am Your friend. Help me to find ways to share that friendship with others. Amen.'

* edwj.org/nd21-29dec1
** edwj.org/nd21-29dec2

Proverbs 9:1–6
'Wisdom has built her house; she has set up its seven pillars. She has prepared her meat and mixed her wine; she has also set her table.' (vv1–2)

The incarnation is God's complete and final invitation to enter into friendship with God. Defined as 'a relationship between two or more friends',* friendship leaves a lot of scope for determining its substance. It takes a lifetime to explore this friendship with God, and presents a series of questions, the answers to which will decide how deep and intimate we allow that friendship to become.

The promises God makes throughout Scripture are many and rich, and require that we let go of things in order to take hold of God's promises in their fullness. This letting go can prove challenging, for we cannot experience the promise before we have released whatever it is that acts as the barrier between us and God.

Deepening our encounter with God always involves leaving. Mary and Joseph left Nazareth, the shepherds left their flock, the wise men left their homeland. King Herod sensed the scale of the interruption that the incarnation in an anonymous cattle shed created. His rejection of the infant King of kings led to a ferocious slaughter as he tried to control the situation (Matt. 2:16).

However, God pre-empted Herod through Joseph's dream. Again Joseph and Mary had to leave, and embrace the discomfort of becoming refugees in Egypt. Realising God's promises comes with consequences that will challenge our preferred way of life and requires that we place our total trust in God.

SCRIPTURE TO CONSIDER: Gen. 12:1–9; Matt. 4:12–22; Luke 19:1–9.

AN ACTION TO TAKE: Leaving always demands that I let go of the familiar and embrace the unknown. Are there habitual patterns of behaviour, ingrained attitudes, or other things it is now time to release?

A PRAYER TO MAKE: 'Lord, help me to embrace my future by obeying You and leaving behind anything that limits my friendship with You. Amen.'

* edwj.org/nd21-30dec

1 Kings 3:4–15

'At Gibeon the LORD appeared to Solomon during the night in a dream, and God said, "Ask for whatever you want me to give you."' (v5)

It's New Year's Eve, a time when well intentioned resolutions are made, yet seldom kept. In contrast, the Christian year traditionally starts with the first Sunday in Advent, so is well and truly up and running by now.

In 1755; John Wesley* introduced the idea of the Christian renewing their commitment to Christ each year with a Covenant Service. He used material from the writings of the seventeenth-century puritans, Joseph and Richard Alleine. With modifications, the Methodist Church still uses this. It's something we can benefit from.

His original Covenant Prayer involved taking Christ as 'my Head and Husband, for better, for worse, for richer, for poorer, for all times and conditions, to love, honour and obey thee before all others, and this to the death'.** Wesley wanted to encourage people to open themselves to God, to take a further step each year in their continuous conversion, a lifetime's process for every disciple.

This is God's invitation: that we grow in our devotion, living every day with Jesus effectively. We learn to listen to God's offer more intently, to consider God's challenge more seriously and choose to make the space to allow God's Spirit to prompt us. This is not just a personal response, but is to be seen as part of the life of faith we are exploring together with all those within our Christian community.

SCRIPTURE TO CONSIDER: Neh. 1:1–11; Dan. 9:1–19; Luke 11:1–13; John 17:1–26.

AN ACTION TO TAKE: You can download a copy of the Covenant Prayer from For you and your Church edwj.org/nd21-31dec1. Read and use it as a prayer but also as a reflection on your Christian life as you enter a new year.

A PRAYER TO MAKE: 'Lord, I am no longer my own but Yours. Help me to live every day with Jesus first, myself last, and others in between. Amen.'

* edwj.org/nd21-31dec2
** edwj.org/nd21-31dec3

COVENANT PRAYER

As we approach the end of the year consider praying this Covenant Prayer on New Year's Eve as you conclude these readings.

I am no longer my own but yours.
Put me to what you will, rank me with whom you will;
put me to doing, put me to suffering;
let me be employed for you, or laid aside for you,
exalted for you, or brought low for you;
let me be full, let me be empty,
let me have all things, let me have nothing:
I freely and wholeheartedly yield all things
to your pleasure and disposal.
And now, glorious and blessèd God, Father, Son and Holy Spirit,
you are mine and I am yours. So be it.
And the covenant now made on earth, let it be ratified in
heaven.
Amen.

Notes

Order form

Get Your **FREE** Daily Bible Reading Notes **TODAY!** (UK ONLY)

Your favourite Bible Reading notes are now available to you for FREE. God has called us back to the original vision of CWR to provide these notes to everyone who needs them, regardless of their circumstance or ability to pay. It is our desire to see these daily Bible reading notes used more widely, to see Christians grow in their relationship with Jesus on a daily basis and to see Him reflected in their everyday living. Clearly there are costs to provide this ministry and we are trusting in God's provision.

Could you be part of this vision? Do you have the desire to see lives transformed through a relationship with Jesus? **A small donation from you of just £2 a month, by direct debit, will make such a difference** Giving hope to someone in desperate need whilst you too grow deeper in your own relationship with Jesus.

4 Easy Ways To Order

1. Visit our online store at **waverleyabbeyresources.org/store**
2. Send this form together with your payment to:
   CWR, Waverley Abbey House, Waverley Lane, Farnham, Surrey GU9 8EP
3. Phone in your credit card order: **01252 784700** (Mon–Fri, 9.30am – 4.30pm)
4. Visit a Christian bookshop

For a list of our National Distributors, who supply countries outside the UK, visit waverleyabbeyresources.org/distributors

Your Details (required for orders and donations)

Full Name:	CWR ID No. (if known):
Home Address:	
	Postcode:
Telephone No. (for queries):	Email:

Publications

TITLE	QTY	PRICE	TOTAL
		Total Publications	

UK P&P: up to £24.99 = **£2.99**; £25.00 and over = **FREE**

Elsewhere P&P: up to £10 = **£4.95**; £10.01 – £50 = **£6.95**; £50.01 – £99.99 = **£10**; £100 and over = **£30**

Total Publications and P&P (please allow 14 days for delivery)	A	

Payment Details

☐ I enclose a cheque made payable to CWR for the amount of: **£** _____

☐ Please charge my credit/debit card.

Cardholder's Name (in BLOCK CAPITALS) _____

Card No. ☐☐☐☐ ☐☐☐☐ ☐☐☐☐ ☐☐☐☐ ☐☐☐☐

Expires End ☐☐ ☐☐   Security Code ☐☐☐

Continued overleaf >>

<< See previous page for start of order form

One off Special Gift to CWR ☐ Please send me an acknowledgement of my gift **B** [　　　]

GRAND TOTAL (Total of A & B) [　　　]

Gift Aid (your home address required, see overleaf)

giftaid it I am a UK taxpayer and want CWR to reclaim the tax on all my donations for the four years prior to this year **and on** all donations I make from the date of this Gift Aid declaration until further notice.*

Taxpayer's Full Name (in BLOCK CAPITALS) _____

Signature _____ **Date** _____

*I am a UK taxpayer and understand that if I pay less Income Tax and/or Capital Gains Tax than the amount of Gift Aid claimed on all my donations in that tax year it is my responsibility to pay any difference.

Your FREE Daily Bible Reading Notes Order

	Please Tick FREE	£2 pcm	£5 pcm	£10 pcm	Other
Every Day with Jesus (1yr, 6 issues)	☐	☐	☐	☐	☐ £____
Large Print *Every Day with Jesus* (1yr, 6 issues)	☐	☐	☐	☐	☐ £____
Inspiring Women Every Day (1yr, 6 issues)	☐	☐	☐	☐	☐ £____

All CWR Bible reading notes are also available in single issue **ebook** and **email subscription** format. Visit **waverleyabbeyresources.org** for further info.

CWR Instruction to your Bank or Building Society to pay by Direct Debit
Please fill in the form and send to: CWR, Waverley Abbey House, Waverley Lane, Farnham, Surrey GU9 8EP

DIRECT Debit

Name and full postal address of your Bank or Building Society

To: The Manager　　Bank/Building Society

Address

Postcode

Name(s) of Account Holder(s)

Branch Sort Code

Bank/Building Society Account Number

Originator's Identification Number

4	2	0	4	8	7

Reference

Instruction to your Bank or Building Society
Please pay CWR Direct Debits from the account detailed in this Instruction subject to the safeguards assured by the Direct Debit Guarantee. I understand that this Instruction may remain with CWR and, if so, details will be passed electronically to my Bank/Building Society.

Signature(s)

Date

Banks and Building Societies may not accept Direct Debit Instructions for some types of account

For a subscription outside of the UK please visit www.waverleyabbeyresources.org where you will find a list of our national distributors.

How would you like to hear from us? We would love to keep you up to date on all aspects of the CWR ministry, including; new publications, events & courses as well as how you can support us.

If you **DO** want to hear from us on email, please tick here [ ] If you **DO NOT** want us to contact you by post, please tick here
You can update your preferences at any time by contacting our customer services team on 01252 784 700. You can view our privacy policy online at waverleyabbeyresources.org